Darkness
Visible

Awakening Spiritual Light through Darkness Meditation

Ross Heaven
and
Simon Buxton

Destiny Books
Rochester, Vermont

Destiny Books
One Park Street
Rochester, Vermont 05767
www.InnerTraditions.com

Destiny Books is a division of Inner Traditions International

Library of Congress Cataloging-in-Publication Data

Heaven, Ross.
  Darkness visible : awakening spiritual light through darkness meditation / Ross Heaven and Simon Buxton.-- 1st ed.
     p. cm.
  Includes bibliographical references.
  ISBN 1-59477-061-1
  1. Spiritual life. 2. Light--Religious aspects. I. Buxton, Simon. II. Title.
  BL624.H382 2005
  204'.46--dc22

                                                              2005023597

Printed and bound in Canada by Transcontinental Printing

10 9 8 7 6 5 4 3 2 1

Text design and layout by Jon Desautels
This book was typeset in Caslon, with Avant Garde Gothic used as a display typeface

For all my children of darkness—my daughters, Mili and Jodie, and my son, Ocean, and my "almost sons" Arran, Rouse, and baby Jaiden. And for Leonard Cohen, poet of the soul, cartographer of the darkworld. I don't think I could run Darkness Visible without your Ten New Songs!

ROSS HEAVEN

To Gwyn Ei Fyd, a true prince of darkness and advocatus diaboli, *to Art O'Murnaghan—the Hibernian Adept—and to Dominic and Jacob, magical children of New Europa.*

SIMON BUXTON

And with thanks from us both to all our students who have made their darkness visible. You allowed us to find the statue within the stone.

Yet from those flames no light, but rather darkness visible.

JOHN MILTON, *PARADISE LOST*

Contents

Inviting the Darkness In

IN AN AGE in the Western world when there is an almost insatiable yearning for "enlightenment," what could be more timely than an invitation to reestablish a sacred relationship with darkness? Indeed, it is in the redefinition of darkness that we discover an entryway into a potent transformational experience that can assist us in rethinking the nature of both reality and healing. What might we learn about ourselves and the powers of the "other world" by surrendering to the beauty and opportunity for greater vision afforded us in darkness?

In all parts of this planet the first nine months of human gestation are spent in the rich, protective darkness of the womb. It is there that the being makes the transition from the spirit world to this one, and it is in the absence of light that the spirits work their greatest magic. It is in the light-absent womb that they do the necessary work to prepare the soul for its journey into life on planet Earth.

In the modern world, the newborn is evicted from the peaceful uterine environment into harsh fluorescent brightness, and it seems that the rest of the person's life is spent trying to sever ties with that nurturing, sensual landscape. In our ever more illuminated houses, streets, and cities, we seem to have lost our way; we have become blinded. We have forgotten the benefits of darkness; we have forgotten how to find our way home. Darkness, however, is ultimately inescapable, and at the end of each day, as the soporific seduction of nighttime overtakes us, we are, once again, transported to yet another gestational experience, yet another opportunity to be reborn.

From a tribal perspective, it is darkness that is the light of the ancestors. It is only in darkness that certain powerful aspects of indigenous technology can be revealed. It is of little surprise, then, that in the African village nearly all rituals of initiation are carried out after the sun has given way to the deep night. The constant presence of darkness provides a protective umbrella that prevents the intrusion of distraction and delusion. It is there that the psyche is invited to surrender to that which is not available in the daylight. It is there that the eyes learn to see what is hidden by the sun's light.

Ross Heaven and Simon Buxton, in a powerful challenge to the popularity of glaringly bright modernity, have discovered and nurtured the most fundamental and fertile ground for the development of true spiritual sightedness. In their workshops, explorations, personal experiences, and writings, they have uncovered the rich resources available only in darkness. Indeed, they have gone so far as to substantiate the clinical benefits of dark-time without negating the importance of acknowledging the mystery—the unknown—that resides in harmony with the measurable. We often find ourselves ill at ease in modern society, caught in recurring cycles of dis-ease and depression. We might ask ourselves whether our discomfort comes from compromising the sacred and balanced partnership between light and dark. What healing might be available to body and soul if we would turn off the lights and invite the powers of the night into our lives?

In the West, there is a largely undiscovered potential that can become a reality only in darkness. What is familiar and sacred to an indigenous person in the nighttime seems, at best, to be an inconvenient irritation to the modern person. The tribal person knows that there are certain types of wounds that can find healing only in the nighttime and only in the hands of the ancestors who show up for work after the last candle has been extinguished.

We would do well to learn to appropriate a definition of an elder as one who is the keeper of the gates of darkness. It is the old who have finally become disillusioned with the glittery brightness of the manufactured world and who feel the enticing whisper of the darkness, inviting them to draw closer to their earlier transitional home, to the place where they were held in their first months, in the deep liquid intimacy of the ancestral womb. It is the sweet power of darkness that invites the discerning listener to attend to the whisperings of the spirit world. In darkness true connection occurs and distraction is no more than a distant, indistinct buzz. *Darkness Visible* invites us to regain our magical vision. Turn out the lights; step into the beauty of darkness.

MALIDOMA PATRICE SOMÉ,
AUTHOR OF *THE HEALING WISDOM OF AFRICA*
AND *OF WATER AND THE SPIRIT*

Journeying Farther Than the Eye Can See

THE VOID, the great vast darkness, is the place before creation. It is described by the Zen Buddhists as empty yet full; the truly fertile, holy ground from which all life is born.

Every autumn plant life falls back into the earth. During the darkness of winter, deep within the earth, new life is always gestating. It is formed in the darkness and then in spring and summer, with the heat of the sun, it bursts forth into great color and beauty.

All life is born out of darkness—including new awareness and new states of consciousness. We all know that our darker states of consciousness bring us to the depths. As we rise out of the depths new awareness is born and our lives take on new meaning.

In indigenous cultures a shaman is a man or woman who sees in the dark. There are cross-cultural shamanic initiations where initiates are placed in darkness for long periods of time. This initiation births the shaman's clairvoyant and hidden healing abilities as a new sense of perception is born. We live in an exciting and powerful time in which many of us are seeking to understand the hidden universe. We are looking to unlock our creative potential. By learning about the power of the darkness we learn how to mobilize "unpotentiated" energy. Just as we dream each night in darkness and awaken to the sun with unlimited potential to create a new day, by doing darkness work we learn how to open our senses and experience the world in a deep, rich, and meaningful way.

As gifted storytellers, Ross and Simon do a brilliant job of inspiring us to learn more about the power of the darkness. They blend cross-cultural stories of initiations in darkness from Europe, Africa, India, Japan, Tibet, North America, South America, and Haiti with scientific findings of how being in darkness affects the brain. I am impressed with how they found a way to bring such a powerful initiation into our modern world. Throughout the book they weave in exercises that they have used in their workshops on darkness and stories from participants about the profound effect this work has had on their lives.

And they don't leave us "in the dark" as we can all try the exercises on our own to awaken new states of awareness and open up to the new perceptions made possible by using our other senses.

Ross and Simon are not just incredible writers; they are also master teachers. They know how to set up a safe space for their workshop participants, which allows for this deep exploration into a new way of seeing. And they have found a way to do the same for their readers.

We all yearn for a deeper and richer way of living and connecting with nature. In *Darkness Visible*, Ross and Simon provide valuable information and exercises to help us make that connection.

So please read on.

SANDRA INGERMAN,
AUTHOR OF *SOUL RETRIEVAL* AND
MEDICINE FOR THE EARTH

Entering Darkness and Seeing the Light

Ceremonial Darkness in the Haitian Vodou Tradition

MY DARKNESS FALLS SUDDENLY and without warning.

One moment I am looking up at the night sky, marveling at the stars scattered like diamonds on a jeweler's velvet, the next I am held from behind with a blindfold across my eyes. Then I am spun three times so I am no longer certain of direction and led into a darkened room, where I will stay for five nights, always in darkness, blindfolded for most of my time there.

This is not a kidnapping. It is a ritual procedure conducted in Haiti as part of the ceremonial process for initiates into Vodou, the Caribbean religion born of African shamanism and carried to the New World in the enslaved hearts and souls of shaman-priests and princes.

A psychologist by training and a writer by profession, I am in Haiti to study Vodou for a book I am writing on traditional spirituality and why it might be needed and important in the modern world.* But Vodou is a

---

*This book, which contains more information on Vodou and my initiation into it, is called *Vodou Shaman* (Rochester, Vt.: Destiny Books, 2003).

secretive religion—not surprising, given the harsh treatment of the slaves who practiced it, many of whom were murdered by their masters simply for praying to their own gods*—and the only way to know it is to be initiated into it and become a priest. This is what I have chosen to do.

Initiation involves a number of ceremonies and warrior trials, most of which are conducted publicly before the village community. But some, like this particular ritual, are different because, once blindfolded, I am required to spend the requisite days in confinement within the sacred space of the *djevo,* the heart of the Vodou temple. During this time, the secret teachings of the religion will be passed on to me and I will be visited by the spirits themselves, feeling them as a presence or, more directly, either through the possession of the priests who oversee this process or perhaps through my own possession. Darkness is central to the experience, and it is the darkness that fascinates me most.

I always imagined that being alone in the dark would be isolating, perhaps even frightening. In fact, my body finds it deeply comforting, though I am aware of my mind working overtime, chewing over questions that, on inspection, seem quite meaningless, and chattering on just to save itself from silence.

There seem to be layers and layers of voices in my head, each one with a personality of its own. Psychologists call these subpersonalities. We imagine ourselves to be one consistent person with a stable worldview, but in fact, if we listen to ourselves, we realize each of us is legion.

I can immediately recognize three such voices in myself. The critic is the first. She speaks with a woman's voice and wants to judge me for getting myself into this situation of potential danger and so many unknowns and for not taking my responsibilities seriously. After all, I have children at home who love and need me. The critic delivers a rage of sarcastic comments— "You've done it again, you fool! You've got yourself into another ridiculous

---

*During the worst days of slavery in the American South, the average black slave could expect to live for thirty years; in Haiti, two years was considered an achievement. Life was cheap and it was often easier to buy a new slave than to deal with one who was causing problems in any way, whether by worshiping an African god or talking in the fields instead of cutting sugar cane.

mess, lying on a dirt floor, blindfolded, in a jungle hut. It's always the same with you; you never learn!"—before she is silenced by another voice, that of the kindly parent, who answers, "Leave him alone. The boy has to learn. He has to experience the world, because that is what being alive is all about!"

Finally there is the voice of the scientist, the impartial observer who walks between both judgments and offers an "informed" and "objective" view of what is actually happening and why. The scientist thinks himself superior to the others because of his objectivity, but it is this very thing that stops him from feeling and distances him not only from the experience but, to some extent, from humanity itself.

To me (whoever "me" is, now that I understand that I am more than one person), this dialogue—with these claims and counterclaims regarding my actions—seems fascinating, until I realize I have been hooked once again by the chatter in my mind and am following this useless and circular discussion in my head instead of experiencing what is actually happening to me right here and now. My head has me trapped in theory and nonsense, keeping me from attending to what *is*.

And then, ironically, I'm back in the cycle as the critic leaps in with her new judgments—"You've done it again, fallen for the game of the rational mind, gotten involved with the voices in your head!"—without realizing that she herself is part of this game. It is quite remarkable how easily we slip into mind-stuff and are lured away from simply being, from feeling something and experiencing our lives.

After a few days of this going around in circles in the darkness, though, something new and surprising happens. My mind, having exhausted itself, perhaps, or having no more visual stimuli to feed and distract it, begins to grow quiet. I notice that the chatter has stopped.

From this point onward I feel an opening up of myself. The priest calls in the spirits, who appear through possession states and offer advice, counsel, divination, and healing secrets or who carry out healings of their own on me. While my rational mind, just a few days ago, would have questioned all of this, I now accept it. In fact, I more than accept it: I feel the healings as they take place. Something shifts in my emotions as I drift in mythological landscapes in the darkness: at a deep, nonrational level I know that of course these healings are real because I experience them as real.

One version of reality tells me that my body is lying on a dirt floor in a squalid hut, but in my mythological mind I am in a great temple, surrounded by gods and goddesses, great pillars of gold, wise elders, visionaries, and master physicians. I no longer know or care which, if either, of these versions is true. What is truth anyway? What is reality? Aren't both simply what we choose to believe?

What I believe right now is that I feel comfortable and comforted here. I am held, loved, supported. I am blissful. This, then, must be the reality of my experience, what is actually happening. I relax even more and drift into dreamscapes. From somewhere I hear the words of Joseph Campbell advising his students to follow their bliss because it is the only way to truth. "The adventure is its own reward."

Hours pass, days—but perhaps they are years or only seconds. In darkness it is hard to tell. This place, this state of being, is as timeless as it is spaceless, with no exact location except in my dreaming mind. But there comes a moment when time returns: my blindfold is removed and I am taken from the djevo and presented to the sun.

This is the first time for days that I have seen nature: the forest, the sky, the earth. Perhaps it is the first time I have ever really seen it, because now everything is alive and different—vast, beautiful, breathing, pulsing, glowing with energy, and singing of its own existence in the hum of cicadas and the whisper of breeze through leaves.

Then, at this most sublime and magnificent moment, I have a Homer Simpson realization: *"Doh! It is alive, you fool!"* And suddenly I see what I have forgotten or not noticed before: Nature is a living thing and I am part of it—creating this vision, created by it. The *it* and the *I* are one.

That grand and inexplicable landscape of mythology that I have been a part of for days (for my whole life, in fact, though I have not been aware of it) is right here in front of me, in the world all around me, the greatest dream of all. The adventure is its own reward.

ROSS HEAVEN

 PREFACE

If Honey, Then Also Sting
Darkness and the Path of Pollen

I said to my soul be still and let the darkness come upon you.

T. S. ELIOT

DARKNESS ARRIVED as a sanctuary for me. I had endured a terrifying and painful initiation into the Path of Pollen, an arcane Keltic* shamanic tradition, at the hands of my teacher and mentor, a Welsh alchemist whose laboratory was his back garden and who carried the formal title of Bee Master.†

The initiation involved being stung in multiplicity on various parts of

---

*The word Keltic is drawn from the archaic word *keltoi*, which we first see applied to the Celts in Greek and Roman writings. The Greeks and Romans came to use it to mean "strangers" or "barbarians" but it is likely that it derives from a Celtic word meaning "secret" or "hidden." We use the word to refer to those within Celtic culture who were—and are—the keepers of hidden wisdom, who concealed the teachings of their lineages by committing nothing—or very little—to writing, relying instead on the oral tradition to safeguard their knowledge. These people existed and exist within Celtic culture, but their tradition is not identical to that of the broader culture. The term is quite different, therefore, from the word Celtic, which has come to denote the Irish, Scots Gaelic, Old Welsh, and Breton races rather than the holders of arcane knowledge, who were the Kelts.

†Fuller and more detailed accounts of my darkness initiation into the Path of Pollen can be found in *The Shamanic Way of the Bee* (Rochester, Vt.: Destiny Books, 2004).

my body by honeybees, the effect of which brought about a transference of my human awareness to that of the honeybee itself, a creature that lives in total darkness within the hive.

Immediately following this initiation, I was taken to a darkened room and placed within a hexagonal handwoven wicker structure some 4 feet in height and 3 feet in diameter, a distinctive shape that encouraged me to assume either a curled, fetuslike position or a squatting, haunched stance with my head slightly bowed. I learned to feel comfortable within this curious structure in the same way a fakir learns to feel comfortable on a bed of nails: a marked unease giving way to unexpected gratitude. Other than the briefest of exits to imbibe my strict diet of fresh pollen and honey, to drink cool spring water, and to relieve myself, I spent the next twenty-three days and nights within this miniature monastic cell.

By entering a prolonged period of darkness, I was making an internal journey from the sunlit side of my valley to the dark side. I had walked through a door in a wall that opened to another world, allowing me to flee the prison house of language and the tyranny of conceptual thinking and literalist intractability. But there was a price to pay for this freedom, for there were challenges on the road ahead. I found myself moving between feeling like a spiritual commando on the one hand and, on the other, perceiving myself as utterly inadequate to my task.

The very first thing that was apparent to me is that when the light of the world goes out, the mind, for a period, goes out too. With this there is a swift return to a primeval condition, a time when darkness was a god as revered and strong as the god of light.

But for me the return to this primeval state was not a smooth one. For an uncounted period of days and nights I was breast-to-breast and mouth-to-mouth with the deepest and most hidden recesses of my self. I was confronted with an orgy of vision and I chased metaphors around sharp corners of dank and stinking tunnels as I moved through a world that carried little or no state of grace.

Learning spiritual methods without introspection brings about one set of problems, but introspection without spirituality brings another. The thousands of practices that are taught within spiritual traditions are no substitutes for self-examination, and this is where the darkness work begins: inner exploration, with darkness serving as a bright mirror. If we fail to know our inner self, crucial aspects of the hidden universe will remain largely inaccessible to us.

A paralysis of the soul followed in the wake of my introspection. The temperature of my existence fluctuated wildly and violently, with no solace of a middle ground. Sometimes the blazing heat from the burn of an invisible sun was so great that I saw and felt the hair on my head catch fire. At other times the north winds of my threatened and fragile ego blew with such an icy ferocity that my limbs would but break.

There were times when my mind seemed to have a mind of its own, contracting and expanding, reminding me of Plato's view of the unconscious as a kind of volcanic activity. My psyche spewed out a flowing furnace of lava and then floated, lost and unmoored, in its dark harbor. Questions rose to the surface: Was my world an invention of my senses? In what kind of physical reality did I live? The darkness unfurled queries about my reality; outer and inner became blurred, floating through a womb of beginnings. I imagined light in its myriad forms and reflected on how it can be manufactured while darkness, technologically, cannot. But in society is not the opposite true? Is it not easier to make darkness than it is to create light?

I felt myself move from being vast in size to microscopically small. My thoughts roamed: Will the scientist always be able to discover ever smaller, more elementary particles inside those we already know, like a never-ending sequence of Russian dolls? Or perhaps there is a smallest thing, a smallest size, a shortest time, where division comes to a full stop on the page. If the universe we live in is of infinite size, anything that has a probability of occurring must occur often, infinitely. I found myself musing, then, that there must be an infinite number of identical copies of me doing precisely what I was doing—contemplating my infinite self!

And furthermore, there must also be an infinite number of identical copies of me doing something other than what I am doing now.

In the wake of great cerebral activity came an internal silence that brought a stilling of the mind, and it was from that place that language once again came to me—but differently than it had before, for from silence, language had less chance of causing divisiveness within me or of becoming stuck in concepts and preconceived notions. Silence disengaged my ego and stopped it from acting reflexively.

All of it changes at evening
Equal to the darkening,
So that night-things may have their time.
Each gives over where its nature is essential.
The river loses all but a sound.
The bull keeps only its bulk.
Some things lose everything.
Colors are lost. And trees mostly.
At a time like this we do not doubt our dreams.[1]

I eventually arrived at the welcoming bosom of the deepest, dream-swirling, charcoal sleep, and from that I awoke to primeval quietude, a place beyond all denomination. With my mind settled into uncommon stillness, I had returned to something akin to the pure consciousness of the very young child who does not differentiate between himself and the world around him. It was here, in this particular place and state, that the work—known within the bee shamanic tradition as Darkness Visible—began in earnest.

I knew when it was time to leave my monastic enclosure—I simply knew, and the first moments of light were a witnessing of the magnificent world as a magical inheritance.

We should enter a country such as this as if it were the embodiment of a more profound level of our own being spread out before us and inviting us to wonder. And from communion with these mansions of the night there endures some direct, supersensual contact, deeper than anything that can be expressed at a rational level. We undertake a ritual plunge into cosmic dreams, the place of the holy unconscious and the parallel universe of the sage, the shaman, and the saint.

According to the theories of aerodynamics, the honeybee should be unable to fly, but our humble, golden friend has not been told this and so continues on its miracle flight. It is in moving beyond the reductive notions that have been placed upon us that we too soar into darkness toward our royal destiny, if we choose to make this flight to freedom.

SIMON BUXTON

1

God in a Time of Darkness

The Spirit beyond the Light

God, at the beginning of time, created heaven and earth. Earth was still an empty waste, and darkness hung over the deep....

GENESIS 1:2

In the beginning there was only darkness everywhere—darkness and water. And the darkness gathered thick in places, crowding together and then separating, crowding and separating....

"THE SONG OF THE WORLD,"
FROM THE PRIMA INDIANS OF ARIZONA

Then God said, Let there be light; and the light began. God saw the light and found it good, and he divided the spheres of light and darkness....

GENESIS 1:3–4

Then he realized, I indeed, I am this creation, for I have poured it forth from myself....

MUNDAKA UPANISHAD

IN THE CREATION myths of the world there is always a time of darkness before the birth of the human race and, within this darkness, an undifferentiated oneness in which God is all and all is God and everything is one. There are no human beings, only God beings, or rather, aspects of God, parts of God—if a unified consciousness can indeed have parts at all—waiting to be born.

And then something happens. God becomes lonely and longs for a partner, a beloved, or, growing curious about his powers and the potentials and possibilities of a god, he wants to know himself. He must separate himself, then, into myriad forms (or, at the very least, one other form) so he can look back at himself and know who he is and what he might be capable of accomplishing. In that Big Bang of consciousness, that explosion into being, all the kingdoms of the world are formed and life as we know it begins.

But God must create not only diversity to know himself; for a God of darkness to see what he is, he must create his opposite: there must be light.

And so with God's illumination come separation and the arrival of opposites, aspects in conflict with one another. The universal consciousness we all knew at one time becomes split into many pieces—into a chaos of fragments, a world unknown, a oneness divided.

"Behold what I have done!" God cries, not so much in awe as in shock at what he has created and the new feelings of loneliness and isolation that begin to well up in him. And so begins the quest of both God and humans to return to the source, to become the void, to find peace and completion and "whole-iness" again.

The prayer of Dionysius the Areopagite, the Bishop of Athens, who was converted to Christianity by St. Paul, reverberates with this longing to return to the darkness before our division, when men might know God once again:

> Direct our path to that topmost height of mystic Lore which exceedeth light and more than exceedeth knowledge, where the pure, absolute and immutable mysteries of heavenly Truth are veiled in the dazzling obscurity of the secret Silence, outshining all bril-

liance with the intensity of their Darkness and surcharging our blinded intellects with the utterly impalpable and invisible fairness of glories surpassing all beauty.

Let this be my prayer. . . . For by unceasing and absolute renunciation of oneself and all things, one shalt in purity cast all things aside and so shalt be led upwards to the Super-essential Ray of Divine Darkness.[1]

This notion of separation and the fate of humans within it can be found in all of the world's religious mythology, whose stories speak of the distance and ambiguity of God (the original first consciousness) from humans (what God has become).

The Greeks regarded human beings as the playthings of the gods, collectively a tiny and insignificant concern to those multiple beings who were often at war with themselves. Jason's voyage on the Argo exemplifies this, with Jason's heroic quest—the search for the golden fleece within the kingdom of the dark—being no more than a chess game between gods who have different agendas and their own points to prove, one of which is that, in the final analysis, humans are incapable of becoming gods.

And yet, Jason *does* succeed.

Our separation from God is also understood in Haitian Vodou. Myths speak of Bondye, the one God, who is so involved in the affairs of the cosmos that he can no longer be appealed to by humans. He does not have the time to care. Instead he provides us with other gods—the Loa, angel-like presences whose task is to keep order and play a sacred part in our lives—as stand-ins for a God who has his own things to worry about. The Loa, in Haiti, are aspects of God, parts of the God energy that suffuses the universe—in other words, God made legion.

In Christian mythology there is also a God who is somewhat unavailable to us, and so we are given angels, archangels, and even fallen angels to keep us company instead.

Sometimes this multiple–God consciousness can seem cruel or at least unfathomable, as God's different personalities war with themselves. The

3

Christian God, who is said to know only love, creates Satan, for example, the epitome of evil. But why would a God who knows only love create evil? How would he even know evil to create it? Yet he creates and then banishes Satan from heaven for daring to love his creator too much. The fallen angel is divided from his father and becomes a god in his own right—the story of every young man's parting from his father repeated throughout time. And so the myth of separation is played out once again.

God's dividedness is evident in the Bible as well. At times he refers to himself as many: "Let us make man, wearing *our* own image; let us put him in command of the fishes of the sea" (Genesis 1:26); "Here is Adam become like one of *ourselves*, with knowledge of good and evil" (Genesis 3:22). At other times he sees himself as a single entity: "Thou shalt have no other God but me."

This contradiction within the God of light is also seen in his actions. He builds a paradise for Adam and Eve, the first human eyes for his experience of the world, and within it plants a tree with beautiful and delicious fruits—and then he forbids his children to eat them! When they inevitably do (because it is in the nature of God to be curious and Adam and Eve are now aspects of God), he is outraged: "Have you eaten of the tree of which I commanded you not to eat?" he bellows.

These words are not so dissimilar from those of Unumbotte, the God of the Bassari people of West Africa, who also gives seeds and fruits to human beings and then leaves them to starve so they have no choice but to eat his gifts. When he discovers their action he rages, "Who told you that you could eat that fruit?"[2] Aristotle's words seem fitting here: "The Gods, too, are fond of a joke."

There is also a less well known Judeo-Christian creation myth that involves the first wife of Adam, a being known as Lilith. Hebraic tradition tells us that Adam marries Lilith because he grows tired of coupling with beasts. But then Lilith tires quickly of Adam and his insistence on sexual obedience, sneers at his sexual crudity, and flies away to make her home by the Red Sea. God sends angels to fetch back Lilith, but she curses them, ignores God's command, and spends her time coupling and then giving birth to a hundred children every day. As a result of this, God must produce Eve, Lilith's more docile (or less hostile) replacement.

Lilith's fecundity and sexual freedom suggests that before she was reborn as Eve in her sanitized biblical form, she was an Earth or mother goddess, a guardian of dark places*—the shadows—and the carrier of a depth-charge wisdom for all of us: *It is for us to enter darkness and eat of the forbidden fruit.*

SEPARATION ANXIETY

We come to God in bits, dismembered. We don't know if the bits can be made to fit in the way they used to. We ask God to re-member us.

MICHAEL BEGG

It is difficult to understand God because his agenda is now divided among all the forms he has become so that not even he is now connected to the source, which was a unified consciousness in which all was understood and the blanket of darkness prevailed.

As a consequence, the natural state of humans has become one of anxiety, of not knowing, of praying for a return to a oneness in which things are understood and all is peace and darkness, as it was before light was sent into the world.

We often see this anxiety reenacted in the life of the growing child. At first he enjoys the sleeping peace of the newborn who knows he is cradled by life, a part of all there is. At this time, he is also blind: before birth, living in the womb, a child does not use his eyes. For some weeks after

---

*Popular Hebrew etymology derives the word *Lilith* from *layil*, meaning "night," the spirit of darkness, whereas Eve translates as "Life" and Adam as "Man." One implication of the Christian rewriting of this creation myth, then, is that man must turn away from darkness in order to embrace life. This is interesting, if confused, religious thinking since, if God did indeed originate in darkness, the suggestion that we must follow the path of the material life and light is, in fact, a turning away from God.

birth his vision is still developing and the muscles involved in sight are still strengthening. His bliss is related to darkness, not to seeing the light.

There soon comes a time, however, when the child realizes he is a unique individual, separate from other human beings and his surroundings: there is an *I* and there is a *You;* there is an *I* and there is a *That.* His eyes see this separation. This is when our fears first begin—with our awareness that we are alone.

Humankind has been searching for reconnection with the infinite and for meaning in life ever since this realization of our aloneness. Most often, if it is serious, this search will take place in darkness, both physical or actual and metaphysical or "the dark night of the soul," as Carl Jung defined it.

Recognizing the primal union that was present in that first darkness before God created light, sages and mystics have always used the dark as a vehicle for returning to a state of bliss and understanding. Whatever name they have for this state—Nirvana, heaven, Gine*—the return to its peace and stillness enables them to break through the concerns and anxieties of their earthly lives, with all of its socially prescribed reality and the conditioning of the world outside, so that they might, in some way, attain reconnection with an undifferentiated consciousness in which all is one once again.

In the solitude of Japanese, Indian, and Tibetan caves, English groves, *fogous,* and *sidhs*—the dark places of the Earth—spiritual seekers have always found solace and the introspection necessary to reflect upon the nature of reality.

Within the Shinto tradition of Japan there is an ascetic discipline known as *komori* (seclusion) that is still practiced today, undertaken in the darkness of a cave, temple, shrine, or even a room in the home that is specially prepared and purified so it may bring the gift of power and illumination. Medieval Japanese ascetics made frequent mention of sojourns in places of darkness such as these and in secluded, windowless huts known as the *komorido,* which can still be found on various holy mountains where seekers undertake their dark retreats.

---

*Gine (pronounced GINN-ay) is the mythical Eden-like Africa of the Haitian Vodou tradition.

The Shinto theory behind the power-giving qualities of this type of seclusion is intriguing: sacred power is seen as manifesting in darkness within a sealed vessel, where it gestates and grows until it eventually bursts through its covering and emerges into the light of the world, a principle illustrated in Japanese myth and folklore wherein supernatural children grow out of fruit or plants and deities appear from gourds.

An interesting parallel is seen in the teachings of the Buddhist spiritual leader Thich Nhat Hanh, who in his poem "The End of Suffering" writes:

> *May the sound of this bell penetrate deep into the cosmos*
> *Even in the darkest spots living beings are able to hear it clearly*
> *So that all suffering in them ceases, understanding comes to their heart*
> *And they transcend the path of sorrow and death.*
> *The universal dharma door is already open*
> *The sound of the rising tide is heard clearly*
> *The miracle happens*
> A beautiful child appears in the heart of the lotus flower.

This quality of an object containing supernatural power in the fruitful darkness it holds within is known as *utsubo*, and the mythic gourds and fruits are its vessels. It is understood that before sacred power—as manifested in a being from another world—can burst its skin and appear in this world, it must first gestate in darkness. Likewise, the aspirant who wishes to acquire spiritual power must undergo gestation in the nearest approximation of an utsubo: a cave, shrine, or darkened chamber. In this womblike stillness he or she fasts and recites prayers and darkness becomes the teacher.

But it is not just in Japan that this search for dark communion takes place. The practice of spending extended periods within caves can also be found historically in the remote peninsula of Land's End in Cornwall, England, for example.

Cornwall is not the only place in Europe where Iron Age communities felt compelled to construct subterranean passages, but there is no evidence that the particular Cornish construction known as a *fogou* ("underground chamber" in Cornish) was in any way imported, and it thus seems likely that it formed part of a local Keltic or pre-Keltic tribal tradition.

The word *fogou* may derive from *ogo*, meaning "cave." Cornish fogous typically consist of a long passage with walls built up in horizontal courses of rough granite stones, typically some 40 to 50 feet long, 6 feet in height, and 5 to 6 feet in width, constructed in a deliberate curve. The chamber was entered through a low restrictive doorway: upon entering, the initiate thus bowed to the darkness.

There is little doubt that the fogou was ceremonial in purpose and formed part of the religious beliefs of the pagan Iron Age. Folk stories passed down through generations describe how fogous were places where treasures lay hidden, guarded by spirits, and where members of witch cults met. During such meetings the passage of the fogou was thought to magically extend itself for miles under land and sea.

Many fogous are aligned to receive the first rays of light from the sunrise at midsummer, the turning point of the solar year. The constructions combine both male and female features in their shape and symbolism: the opening to the fogou represents the uterus or womb of the Earth and the rays of the sun symbolize the erect male organ, which is received at the perfect moment for impregnation and the creation of life—the spiritual awakening of those who gestate in its moist depths.

This further suggests a cult of chthonic deities of death and rebirth wherein *del congresso notturno del lammie* (the midnight gathering of witches) occurred, with its lurking ancestral spirits and archaic divinities. The traditional "witching hour," when these cult members gathered, is a liminal period or "crack" between the old day and the new. Midnight is the mystical time of the in-between, when things return to their primeval source and the gates between the worlds lie open. The clock stops between the first stroke of midnight and the last, and at this moment we can explore the twilight dimensions of consciousness and the concealed regions of the spirit, where the divine heights and animal depths of the soul entwine.

In a similar way, Raymond Moody, author of *Life after Life* and *The Light Beyond,* talks of the ancient oracle sites of Greece, called *psychomantions,* which usually feature dark caves and labyrinthine subterranean passages where visitors may explore and experience heightened states of awareness in which their own inner knowing and divinatory powers may be stimulated or, indeed, their ability to speak with the dead. One of these sites, the Oracle of Poseidon (also known as the Oracle of Souls) near Sparta, for example, also contains a tunnel, now covered over, which was said to lead to the Kingdom of the Dead.

In an interview in *Fortean Times* Moody relates how he noticed a stone bowl in one of these psychomantions that he reasoned had once contained oil or water, providing a reflective surface in the midst of the darkness, which the visitor would gaze into in order to call up the souls of the dead. When Moody experimented with this phenomenon by building his own psychomantion in a dark-walled, dimly lit room, with only a mirror or bowl of water for reflection, his subjects experienced a reunion with a departed loved one in 153 out of 155 cases, and around 30 percent also heard the voices of the dead.[3]

On the other side of the world, among the Dagara tribe of Burkina Faso in Africa, the darkness is also sacred. Indeed, in common with other proto-historical tribes, the Dagara forbid any illumination of the darkness, for light is known to scare away the sprits. Night is considered the "daytime" of these spirits and of the ancestors whose task it is to tell the Dagara what lies upon their life paths. Shedding light upon the darkness is thus akin to an insult to the spirits—a choice to ignore the opportunity they offer for real illumination. To the Dagara, this is inconceivable.

When Malidoma Somé, who was born a Dagara but was abducted and raised at a Jesuit mission, returned to his tribe fifteen years after being taken away, he discovered that no one in the village wanted any form of light, and that the villagers were expected to function in the dark.* "I was given light

---

*The only exception to this is the light from a bonfire, which, although it emits a powerful glow, is not prohibited as there is always drumming around the fire and the beat of the drum is known to cancel out the light.

because I had lost the ability to deal with darkness, and each time people saw the timid light of the shea-oil lamp in my room, they would walk away from it as if it signaled the presence of someone playing with the elements of the cosmos. No young man ever came to sit by me at night."[4]

The Lakota Sioux of North America also regard darkness as the home of the spirits. The most powerful healing ceremony, still conducted by Lakota shamans, is the *yuwipi*, which translates as "they wrap him up."

The ceremony takes place in a room that has been totally darkened. The shaman's hands are bound together behind his back and he is enveloped in a blanket that is wrapped tightly around him so he resembles an Egyptian mummy. He then lies down on a bed of sage and, during the healing, is freed from his bonds by spirits that appear in the darkened room as tiny flashes of blue light.

Other phenomena experienced during similar rituals (which have also all been reported by students on our Darkness Visible retreats) include the sound of birds flying around the room; voices, often choral; and the sound of rattles moving through the air, sometimes hitting the floor or ceiling violently and giving off flashes of bluish light. These phenomena can be alarming but are considered highly auspicious by the Lakota, for they indicate the level of spiritual power that is present and that can bring about healing miracles.

Within the Bon tradition of Tibet, a detailed system of working in darkness has also survived intact. Bon is Tibet's oldest spiritual tradition and, as the indigenous source of Tibetan culture, has played a unique role in shaping the country's identity. Within it, the faithful practice a forty-nine-day darkness retreat during which they withdraw from external stimuli in order to reveal a path to totally entering into the self.

During this darkness practice, after an initial period, the subjective sensation of time begins to change. Vision arrives and with it rays of light, rainbows, and symbols. Landscapes open up and the visions become more pronounced, as Bon teacher Tenzin Wangyal Rinpoche reports of his own darkness retreat:

The first vision came during the second morning session of the second week. While I was in a state of contemplation I saw the huge, bodiless head of Abo Tashi Tsering before me in space. The head was enormous. The first few seconds I was afraid, and I then resumed my practice. The head remained in front of me for over half an hour; the vision was as clear as that of normal everyday external reality, and at times even clearer.[5]

While keeping ceremonial silence, the Bon practitioner receives lectures and talks from his teacher, an aspect of the practice that is also consistent with the Path of Pollen, whose students are given Knowledge Lectures during their time in silence. In both cases, teaching is imparted in darkness to a mind that is still, receptive, and alert.

Every day my master Lopon would come and sit outside the retreat hut and talk with me for half an hour. It was very important for me to be close to the master during this time. I could not remember all the teachings in advance, and as I had to change practices and visualizations every week, he would instruct me on these as appropriate.

My mind was very void, empty and without concepts during the times of practice; my experience was that is was good not to receive external information such as news. News creates a disturbance, giving rise to whole successions of thoughts that distract the mind from the practice.[6]

Such a time of inner seeking is also part of the initiatory practices of Haitian Vodou. The shaman-to-be is blindfolded when he or she enters the djevo—the sacred inner sanctuary of the church where the most secret teachings are imparted by the priests and the spirits themselves—and remains in darkness for the first few days of his or her initiation.

This practice, although considered African in origin, may also have been at least partly influenced by the beliefs of the Taino people, who were indigenous to Haiti long before the African slaves or their Spanish and French masters arrived.

The Taino believed that the sun and moon come out of caves and that all people once lived in caves as well, emerging from them only at night, lest the sun should transform them. This nocturnal life also extends to the souls of the dead, who go to Coaybay, the underworld, where they rest by day and come out at night in the form of bats.

The initiate who leaves the dark cave of the djevo is first presented to the sun, which is regarded as a saint in its own right with the power of transformation and healing. The initiate has been reborn again as a child and must enter the world anew in order to truly understand it: from darkness comes light. When he or she emerges from the djevo, the initiate sees the world afresh through eyes washed clean by the dark, and the first thing he or she must look upon is the sun.

Modern science also has its own creation myths, of course, and, interestingly, since science so often seems at war with spirituality, these are also centered on a darkness that was once unified before the light came in and we entered a world of confusion.

"A small group of physicists is battling what they see as the cosmological equivalent to the bogeyman: an enormous dark force, that nobody has ever seen, driving galaxies apart," reported Reuters Wire Service on March 22, 2005.[7]

> Conventional wisdom holds that the mysterious force, called "dark energy," may make up 70 percent of the universe, and could be the determining factor in whether it is eventually destroyed billions of years from now. But Italian and American cosmologists are offering a controversial alternative to explain the accelerating expansion of the universe. They say it's not dark energy, but an overlooked after-effect of the "Big Bang"—which cosmologists believe gave birth to the universe.[8]

According to this new mythology (for all myths are simply what we choose to believe or truths that carry resonance for us), "the forces of the universe can be explained by 'long ripples' from the Big Bang itself, the implications of which would be 'infinite drift and cosmic darkness.'. . . That could include changes to theories about the ultimate fate of the universe, particularly whether it will collapse in a 'big crunch,' be completely blown apart in a 'big rip,' or just drift steadily until galaxies are so far away from each other they cannot be seen—in effect taking stars from the sky."[9]

For our scientists, darkness—"dark energy"—was also present before creation and our options as human beings are to go back to the darkness (the big crunch), expand further, metaphorically speaking, into more light and the big rip of increasing separation, or simply to drift.

The myths of our scientists are no different in this respect from those of our distant ancestors huddled around fires in their caves or the leaders of our ancient and enduring traditions of the spirit. Somewhere for us all, darkness holds the answers to our being and our destinies.

THE SACRED IN THE PROFANE

Men searching for the historical Jesus look into a deep, dark well,
see a reflection of themselves, and call it "Lord."

ALBERT SCHWEITZER

The discoveries from this broad spectrum of religious encounters with darkness—whether those of a Vodou or Shinto priest, a Dagara tribesman, or a member of a medieval witch cult—are now also edging into mainstream neuroscience. Theories about exactly what occurs during transcendental states are becoming increasingly sophisticated, with a recognition that there are common brain pathways underlying all mystical states and that it is only the cultural interpretations of these that vary.

The experience of darkness, our scientists tell us, is not culture-centric but goes beyond the forms of darkness used into something deep and primal within all of us. In mythic terms, this may be our remembrance of God, of who we once were before we decided to know ourselves, in which process we lost ourselves. During retreats into darkness like those discussed above, there is an opportunity to purify the self, to shake off the socialized and separated mind, and, simply, to *re-member*—that is, to bring ourselves back together. We go into the dark to bring forth our light in the knowledge that when we suppress any feeling or impulse, we also suppress its opposite.

> *Thus our life is under death, love of ourselves under hate of ourselves, glory under ignominy, salvation under perdition, justice under sin, strength under infirmity, and universally every one of our affirmations under its negation.*
>
> MARTIN LUTHER

If we deny our ugliness, we lessen our beauty. If we deny our fear, we minimize our courage. If we deny our greed, we reduce our generosity. If we deny the God within, then our humanity is also lost.

Freud tells us that a negation is as good as an affirmation and that what we sense or present of ourselves on the surface is profoundly linked to its opposite. In the psyche, then, only our contradictions tell us truth—the light within the darkness and the dark within the light—and our task as human beings is to integrate these opposing forces so that these energies can flow more freely.

Darkness practice may assist us in this integration, producing psychological insights, spiritual illuminations, and the experience of repressed material and unusual phenomena, such as remarkably lucid levels of uncommon consciousness, in which the borders between dreaming and not dreaming diminish or disappear altogether. What it always does is heal. The chatter of the mind ceases and we are able to explore our luminosity, experiencing the world as we all first saw it: as a sea of energy beyond the forms of all that surrounds us.

The student of darkness becomes a poet of the soul and explorer of the infinite. In darkness, we become seers—those who witnesses the world not with eyes, but with the entire body. From this physical darkness, psychological and metaphysical insights may arise, spiritual practices may deepen, and we may come to know God. A sustained calm and quietude in the challenges of our daily lives may be truly and fully embraced when we close our eyes to the light.

> **Note:** The exercises found at the ends of the chapters throughout this book are practices you can undertake if you wish to explore darkness work to see what information might be available to you within your own dark world of the inner mind. There is, of course, no compulsion to complete any of these exercises and you can skip them if you like. But if you do decide to try them, we think you might find them . . . illuminating.

TRY THIS
◐ Close Your Eyes

The first step in darkness work is simply to experience the dark, but actively instead of passively. We all experience darkness, of course, every time we blink or lie down to sleep. But most of us think of these as interruptions in our normal life of doing things in the world—if we think of them at all. Blinking is, after all, an automatic function and sleep is something we have to engage in each day.

To become a voyager into darkness, try spending some time with your eyes closed, as if in meditation, and simply be aware of what thoughts, images, and other information start to surface. You may never have noticed any of these before because your attention was so firmly trained on the world "out there." At first, you might even find it a discipline simply to keep your eyes closed.

Starting small is recommended—no more than fifteen minutes at a time—but you can build up to longer periods of an hour or more. Then, when you are comfortable with the darkness, try moving or dancing in the dark. How do these taken-for-granted activities feel now that you are using your other senses to guide you?

◖◗ Inviting the Darkness: The Interior Stars

As an extension of the exercise above, the following technique from the Path of Pollen serves dual purposes, as both an invitation to darkness and a method for stimulating the art of *seeing* in the dark by activating power centers—interior stars—that reside in the palms of the hands.

The first step is to rub the hands together purposefully for a minimum of two minutes with increasing speed and intensity. Doing this generates heat, which stimulates the interior stars.

As soon as you stop rubbing your hands together, place your palms over your eyes, keeping them slightly cupped so they do not touch the eyes or eyelids.

Now close your eyes and adjust your palms so they exert a very slight vacuum on the eye sockets. This can be tested by withdrawing one or both hands from the eyes and at that moment feeling the sensation of a gentle airlock.

Ensure that your eyes are covered completely, not by the fingers, but by the palms. This can be tested by opening the eyes and gazing into the center of your palms. What you should see is an inky black darkness, a vast landscape ahead, void of light, but warm and inviting. Do not exert pressure on your eyeballs as this will merely produce *phosphenes*—internal light patterns.

Without any expectations, allow yourself to move into the dark amorphous landscape ahead of you—the kingdom of the midnight sun—and explore this for a minimum of five minutes, extending the journey by five minutes on each further occasion, to a maximum of three hours.

◖◗ Playing God

The religious texts of the world tell us that there was a time before separation when we all knew the mind of God because we were part of that mind. And then God decided to experience himself, and one creative mind became many different souls. You are one of those souls.

With your eyes closed, allow to form within you an image or sensation of what this primal Godlike state would have been like for you when you were a part of a conscious and undifferentiated energy. Feel how it is to be part of this soul community. Drift with it for a while.

At some point, you decided to separate from this energy so that you could be born and experience life as yourself, one form divided from the whole. What was your purpose for doing this? What did you come here to explore? When you consider your life now, have you fulfilled this purpose or, if not, what is there still to do?

◐ Forgiving God

In therapeutic practice, clients often seek healing because of some schism or great divide in their life. They feel alienated, lost, or apart from someone, or perhaps someone significant in their lives did not love them enough or in the way they wanted. This person who gave too little or the wrong kind of love might present as a parent or partner, but beneath this there often may be a greater existential separation: the client feels alone.

That feeling is valid. Since the time when we fell from grace and were thrown out of Eden, we have all been alone. The first person to forgive, then, is God—or, if you prefer, the essence of life itself—for having created your isolation.

Close your eyes and let emerge an image of whatever you consider God or life itself to be, along with your relationship to it. It doesn't matter in the slightest what form this image/being takes. Talk to this being, expressing honestly everything you need to say about the unjustness of the situation in which you find yourself and the rejection and abandonment you feel, being sure to include your grief, rage, and fear, as well as your joy.

And then change your place: become God or life itself and look back at yourself. Then, from this perspective, answer your own complaints. Let God explain to you why things are this way.

Then switch again, becoming yourself. Do you believe God? If not, continue with this dialogue, changing places when you need to, until you reach some understanding and agreements for the future.

When you are ready to forgive, step back from this image and see yourself and God facing each other as separate beings, then allow the two of you to walk toward and into each other so your two beings merge and become one image of a new God-Self.

Breathe in the energy of this union and see it as a light that fills your heart.

I often think the job of man is not to find God but to become him.

ERICH FROMM, *THE ART OF LOVING*

The Tunnel at the End of the Light

The Practice of Darkness

*Mystery and imagination arise from the same source. This source is
called darkness. . . . Darkness within darkness, the gateway
to all understanding.*

LAO-TZU

WE ARE ALL familiar with the Icarus myth: A boy creates a magical
pair of wings from bee's wax and feathers, and begins to fly. He flies higher
and higher despite his father's warnings, continuing ever upward toward
the light of the sun. He is consumed by his drive toward the light until the
wax in his wings begins to melt in the sun's heat, his feathers drop away,
and he falls into the Aegean Sea and drowns.

We might sum up the moral of this tale in this way: "Too much light
and your wings may be lost." Yet within the religious traditions of many
denominations there is often a largely unbalanced emphasis on embracing
light and following a sole trajectory of ascension. As the myth of Icarus
informs us, though, the inevitable curse and course of those who chase
spiritual light is that they must eventually fall back down to Earth. In less

mythic terms: The more we walk toward the light, the longer our shadows grow behind us. The route back to the source, then, is not upward to the light, but downward into darkness.

When Buddha realized enlightenment, he touched the earth—a simple gesture reaffirming his connection to our physical, planetary home. Putting "pennies in our shoes" is the analogy mythologist Joseph Campbell came up with to translate the actions of the Buddha—and is something we all may need to do to counter being taken ever upward in our spiritual pursuits and disciplines.

The philosopher Pliny also remarked that for every step toward the light there must be an equal and opposite step into the darkness. He knew that for every branch of every tree to be secure in high winds, the trees themselves must be firmly rooted within the dark earth, anchoring all that rises up toward the sun. Before the temple is built, he informs us, we must dig downward to secure its foundations.

The vast majority of indigenous spiritual traditions of the world contain this safeguard. Those within these most time-tested traditions know well the potential pitfalls and challenges attached to seeking to step into a greater intimacy with the supernal realms of the gods—and darkness is the tool they use as both a means to this interaction and a safeguard for the journey.

We might say that darkness, when encountered mindfully, can become the most potent spiritual tool we have at our disposal—a statement that seems all the more remarkable because the power of darkness in this context is so rarely talked of, written about, or taught. In fact, historically, such use of physical darkness was embraced only by the most advanced practitioners.

It is said that the best place to hide something is in plain view—and how much more plain could the opening to darkness be for us, present as it is every time we blink and every day when the sun goes down? Every night, as sun sets, the darkness descends and we may choose to allow our perception of everything around us to be altered, for after darkness falls all cats become leopards.

Most people, however, are quick to dismiss the power of the ubiquitous: its potency often goes unseen by the novice and is not explained by the master. Something that is as common as darkness is seen as holding no value and is often ignored, its potency obscured as the seeker searches for more complex, obtuse, and obscure means to arrive at his or her royal destiny.

Yet all we need do is close our eyes.

THE MODERN SEARCH FOR MEANING

*One thing that comes out in the myths is that at the bottom of
the abyss comes the voice of salvation. The black moment is the
moment when the real message of transformation is going to come.
At the darkest moment comes the light.*

JOSEPH CAMPBELL, *REFLECTIONS ON THE ART OF LIVING*

Darkness work is truly cross-cultural. It can be found within Taoist teachings dating back 2,500 years and can be traced to Buddhist, Christian, Hindu, aboriginal, ancestral, and indigenous traditions. Within many paths and faiths it is considered a secret—a staggering one that is kept hidden by its very prevalence, for darkness is simultaneously everywhere and nowhere.

In many traditions darkness is used to mark the very start of a person's induction into spiritual advancement. Within these initiatory practices, the length of time an initiate remains in darkness varies from culture to culture, from just a few hours to a staggering nineteen years.

The experience of shamans and seekers engaged in introspection in dark caves may seem a million miles away from our contemporary life, but there is something within darkness—its healing essence or mythic quality, perhaps—that endures, even today, as a source of illumination and even miracles.

The singer Johnny Cash once spoke of a time in his life when he felt lost and alone, abandoned by God and separated from his purpose:

> I was scraping the bottom of the filthy barrel of life. I hadn't slept in days and I was taking amphetamines and sleeping pills by the

handful—the sleeping pills just to keep from shaking from the amphetamines. . . . I was down to 160 pounds, maybe 155. . . . I was just walking death. I was disgusted with myself.[1]

Instinctively, he was drawn to darkness, the Nickajack Cave on the Tennessee River. "When I went into the cave, it was because I didn't want to see the light of day ever again. I'd decided I would go in there and let God take me away and put me wherever he had to put people like me," he said.[2]

The Nickajack Cave is now flooded and inaccessible but was once vast, with huge underground chambers that were the camping grounds of Confederate soldiers during the Civil War and, before that, the home of the Nickajack Indians. Deep within the caves there are ancient burial grounds and it was here that Cash lay down to die, next to the skeleton of an old Indian.

> But something happened. It was like, all of a sudden, a peace came over me. At first I rejected it because it was a feeling of sobriety, which seemed impossible because I'd taken so many amphetamines to finish myself off, but there it was: Lying there, I got totally straight and sober.
>
> Then I became aware of where I was with God and the feeling came to me that he wanted to speak to my heart. I got the message that I wasn't in control of my destiny, God was, and his will was that right now I had to live, not die. I felt the overpowering urge to get up on my knees and start crawling.[3]

The cave was pitch black, a labyrinth with many passages leading off its chambers and perilous drops into vast caverns, but Cash kept crawling blindly, driven by instinct, until at last he saw the light of the outside world through the cave entrance. It was as if his trajectory was directed by—or perhaps toward—God.

As he emerged, Cash discovered another miracle. For no apparent reason his wife, June, and his mother were both waiting for him, sent there by whispers of intuition and the voices of spirits. His mother had driven all the way from California. "I knew there was something wrong with you," she said. "I had to come to Tennessee to find you."

"Well, momma, I've been in bad shape but I'm ready to start trying to take care of myself; I'm ready to commit," said Cash. His wife had a basket of food for him and he "ate and drank like a pig" for the first time in weeks. "Then they took me home."[4]

DARKNESS VISIBLE RETREATS

For a number of years, we have run Darkness Visible retreats and workshops in which participants live in total blackout for a period of five days or more. Their experiences suggest that darkness is potent as a means of accessing the infinite, just as it has always been and just as Cash found it to be. These are a few of their comments:

It was the most incredible, fulfilling experience ever. . . . The darkness has given me so much—the courage to face my journey in life with a faith I never had or knew I could possibly achieve before. It has been life-changing for me.

Amazing. I still can't find the words to describe the experience, nor am I fully aware of all the implications it will have on my life. It was a truly sacred time.

My heart feels like it's cracked wide open. It was truly an amazing experience, the effects of which are still happening now and will reverberate on and on.

The darkness was incredibly powerful. We did things that I would not have thought possible for sighted people plunged into blindness. As individuals, our differences fell away when we were blind. Perhaps it had to do with us all being vulnerable together, so the only thing possible was to give love, understanding, compassion, and acceptance. If in our society we could all recognize that even with our eyes open we are all vulnerable together, the world might become a more loving place.

Before now, I've known in my head only that we are spiritual beings who inhabit physical bodies, that our spirits are connected, that all is one, that the universe we occupy is pure, loving energy. Now I *know* that the energy of love that is the universe is organized, and it wants to help each of us. All we have to do is trust, step into its path, and allow it to show us the way. The effects continue to manifest as I write this, weeks after the workshop finished, and I'm sure they will continue to do so. I find myself returning regularly to darkness and to the energy of our group for sustenance.

MASTERS OF MYTH AND MAGIC

In a dark time, the eye begins to see,
I meet my shadow in the deepening shade.

THEODORE ROETHKE, "IN A DARK TIME"

Shamans are the ancient masters of myth and magic. Described by anthropologist Mircea Eliade as "walkers between worlds," their gift is to see that which is invisible to others. Indeed, the very definition of the word *shaman* is "he or she who possesses the ability to see in the dark."

Shamans understand that anything seen in darkness or with eyes closed is a message from the spirit, whatever we conceive this spirit to be—an inner power that we can draw upon for guidance and inspiration, an external force, or an energy of universal consciousness. For the shaman, every image seen in the mind's eye has meaning, resonance, and purpose in our life, and all that we sense holds information. Rather than ask about the nature of what we see or sense in our mind—whether it is real (which it must be, by virtue of our sensing it at all)—we must focus our attention on the perception itself, whatever it is that we sense, so we can allow it to serve as another source of information.

Shamanism is animistic in its worldview, for shamans have always known that everything is alive and has spirit. Where such knowledge endures, its power is felt in a very real way. *Yahoo! News* recently carried a story, for example, about the aboriginal Onge (pronounced OHN-ghee) tribe of India, who were able to survive the 2004 tsunami in Asia because of their spiritual attunement to nature.

> When the water in the creek suddenly ran out to sea on the morning of December 26 [the Onge] knew the evil spirits were up to no good.
>
> They scattered pig and turtle skulls around their settlement and hurled stones toward the ocean. Hurriedly gathering their baskets, bows and arrows, they then fled into the jungle, bearing amulets of ancestral bones for protection.
>
> Minutes later, the tsunami that left nearly 300,000 people dead or missing in the Indian Ocean region slammed into their tribal reserve in India's remote Andaman islands. All 96 Onge survived, even as residents of the nearby town of Hut Bay perished.[5]

Researchers believe that the Onge migrated from Africa during the Stone Age, thirty thousand to sixty thousand years ago, carrying with them their traditions and their knowledge of the spirit world. They survived the tsunami because of their understanding of how nature works and their awareness that water disappearing from their creek could mean only danger.

"The water went away very quickly, and, like breathing in and out of the body, the sea water had to come back very rapidly and in a big way," Totanagey, an Onge man, explained to anthropologist Vishvajit Pandya. "We saw the water and knew that more land would soon become covered with sea, and angry spirits would descend down to hunt us away."

The Onge reacted instantly to the threat, guided by their knowledge of these spirits. As they fled, they threw rocks behind them, so the spirits would look for the tribe where the rocks landed, instead of in the jungle, where they hid.

The people finally learned that they had succeeded in warding off the spirits when, eight days later, a tribeswoman gave birth to a baby girl and their number grew to ninety-seven.

Often, for tribes such as these, the spirit of darkness is the oldest in all existence. It is the great power that holds an astonishing intelligence within its vastness—and that we may draw upon in the modern world. Even if we do not believe in spirits, when darkness descends, the spirits believe in us.

THE CHALLENGE OF DARKNESS

In the early part of the twenty-first century, a somewhat unusual restaurant, Dans le Noir (In the Dark), opened in Paris. In this establishment, the customer eats in darkness and is served by blind waiters.

"It awakens the other senses," remarked the restaurant owner, Edouard de Broglie. "It alters [your] perspective and your relations with others. It shows what happens when you can't see and allows you to explore new sensations." He added that he believed the lack of visual contact with what is on our plate can give entirely new meaning to food and to the sensation of eating.

The restaurant has seven blind people serving fifty-five diners in total darkness—literally, the blind feeding the blind. Eyes wide open or eyes shut, diners sit in an inky blackness to which their eyes can't adjust.

Similar establishments have now opened in Zurich and Berlin and, over the past few years, other experiences involving darkness and the sensations it causes have been staged at various arts and theater festivals.

But even such a gentle encounter with darkness as dining in it is a challenge for modern humans. Why? Perhaps because we have become so blinded by the daylight—by the assault on our senses of ten thousand advertisements and television soap operas until even our hearsay is made up of plots within plots from old movies or TV shows. In darkness there is none of this and our blindness can unfold to become a way of true seeing—into ourselves, our purpose, and the nature of reality beyond the media smokescreen of socially conditioned reality.

But also important is how or why we enter into darkness—that is, the intention we carry behind our decision to be enveloped by its mantle. This is well illustrated by Brian Keenan, who went to Beruit in 1985 and made headline news when he was kidnapped by the fundamentalist Shi'ite militia and held in the suburbs of the city for four and a half years, much of this time in darkness. He has written movingly about his plight and the impact of darkness upon his psyche and well-being during this time.

> I have been and seen the nightmare exploding in the darkness. I am in the charnel house of history, I am ash upon the wind, a screaming moment of agony and rapture. I have ceased being. I have ceased becoming. Even banging my body against the wall does not retrieve me to myself.[6]

Somehow these words are reminiscent of Michael Begg's on page 5: "We come to God in bits, dismembered. . . . We ask God to re-member us." Darkness presented within a terrifying environment such as the one Keenan experienced will bring terror. It creates a very real and reasonable fear.

Though darkness entered into as a sacred action, with a view to embracing ourselves with the arms of wholeness, may invoke shadow and associated terrors, with this sanctity of intent and an atmosphere of support, we may be able to transmute the power of this shadow and facilitate an extension and expansion of the soul. This has been our experience during our Darkness Visible retreats.

On these retreats, the effects of prolonged darkness are unique for each person, relating directly to the life story of each and the "myth" of who each individual believes him- or herself to be. Concurrently but at a deeper level (the level of what we might call the "myth of humankind"), however, the effects of darkness are quite consistent among all those who step into its work. They include the attainment of renewed energy and the ability to move past self-limitations, to meet life's challenges with greater ease, and to face the unknown without fear, as participants' comments above suggest. (See pages 23–24.)

Besides environmental or social reasons for the impact of darkness upon us, there are also biochemical effects feeding our transcendent experiences. It is fascinating to conjecture that our distant ancestors knew of these not through the proofs and mathematics of science, but through their direct awareness of changes within—one of countless examples, perhaps, of the claim that shamans were not only the first doctors, healers, artists, and poets, but also the first scientists.*

In the brain, the neurotransmitter seratonin—which enables us to inhabit normal waking consciousness, to see reality as it is normally experienced—is produced in reaction to light. In darkness, however, melatonin is produced instead and is then converted into pinoline, a biochemical involved in dreaming consciousness, so that we see reality in a wholly uncommon way.

Once pinoline is released into the brain, the production of DMT (dimethyltryptamine) is stimulated. DMT represents the body's natural ability to create any reality we choose and is also one of the main ingredients of many psychotropic plants such as the visionary Amazonian vine used in the preparation of ayahuasca, believed to create in those who take it telepathic states and communion with spirit and with the world beyond differentiated forms. Being in darkness naturally stimulates the brain's production of DMT and will therefore lead automatically to a new experience of reality.†

Through DMT, the stranglehold of the rational mind is dissolved and we focus on the present moment, of which we are a part. We are at one with the spiritual injunction to be here now, in touch with the full range of

---

*For a recent example of the model of shaman as first scientist, see the work of Dr. Michael Winkelman of the Department of Anthropology, Arizona State University, in particular his recent publication *Shamanism: The Neural Ecology of Consciousness and Healing* (Westport, Conn.: Bergin & Garvey, 2000).

†In this context, it is interesting that ayahuasca, the visionary brew of the Amazon people, whose spiritual tradition acknowledges no division between humans and God, is now classified as an illegal drug in the United States. This is because of the DMT it contains, which is also an illegal

our senses, wholly and completely ourselves. We are thereby able to move into a new and different future, one that we envision and create, rather than one created from the dictates and definitions of others who have led us to this moment in time and to our very need for darkness to reconnect us with all we once knew before we were told what we should believe.

GOING INTO THE DARK

There are three common phases to the initial experience of darkness: First, we experience a period of adjustment during which the conditioned mind is at war with what we call the mythological or connected mind, the "DMT mind" within us that is capable of remembering the oneness of the world. This period is characterized symbolically by our experience of God's dividedness, where the critic, the kindly parent, and the scientist (among other aspects) fight for control of our thoughts and perceptions and our experience of reality.

Next, the mental chatter stops and we begin to feel an intimate intensity that reduces the mind to silence. From this silence comes a rush of intuitive images, archetypes, abstract forms, and colors, all of which may contain symbolic, metaphorical, metaphysical, or poetic information about who we are and what we have become. This second stage can feel like an opening up of the soul, as if we are on our way back to the primal oneness that we remember in our souls and cells. We experience a sense of awe at our simple existence. Space opens up and begins to grow. This stage is not so different from descriptions of the ayahuasca or DMT experience, which, according to Wade Davis, involves "astonishing visual imagery. The sensation is rather like being shot out of a rifle barrel lined with baroque paintings and landing in a sea of electricity."[7]

---

psychedelic. This regulation is curious given that every human brain naturally contains DMT, a chemical that enables us to perceive reality as different from the socio-political terms in which it is defined and presented to us. The symbolic message behind the classification of these substances as illegal, therefore, seems to be: "We do not want you to have access to your own powers of vision, but rather to accept the world and your life only as we present it to you."

In the third and final phase, we enter blackout, a state of mind in which we are completely without thought but absolutely present, right here, in the infinite Now. At this point a deep peace descends and, instead of sinking into mental chatter and a flood of images, we relax into a world of pure energy. This is the world we knew as infants, before our conditioning took over, a world where forms and shapes are fluid and without structure, for it is only our habitual way of seeing things that gives them shape and meaning at all.

In our Darkness Visible retreats, the arrival of the blackout stage is quite evident. A hush descends on the room, which strangely seems to grow darker. The energy in the group changes. The calm of darkness seems contagious; we can actually watch it moving round the room, from person to person, like a sigh on a breath. As Bid Ben Bid Bont, a Bee Master in the European initiatory Path of Pollen, has said, "Fruit ripens slowly but falls suddenly."*

For those pursuing darkness work, these three phases exist outside of linear time. No stage takes a set number of minutes to either reach or experience in full, but instead may be experienced irregularly, each taking minutes or hours depending on our individual interaction with the dark, our resistance or surrender to the process, and our engagement with the images that begin, almost immediately, to bubble up from our unconscious mind once the outside world is removed and our eyes turn inward to the soul.

We should feel no rush to experience or pass through these stages. Each phase will arrive eventually; all we need do is relax. Again, from the Bee Master Bid Ben Bid Bont: "It is not how busy you are, but why you are busy. The bee is praised, the mosquito swatted."

Many spiritual disciplines take their initiates through these stages toward a realization of God and the seamless energetic universe, and in many of them darkness is used as the vehicle for this journey. In Haitian Vodou, blindfolds are wrapped around the initiates' eyes as they complete the first cycle of initiation, the *bat guerre* —the "battle for the spirit." The bat guerre

---

*See Simon Buxton, *The Shamanic Way of the Bee.*

is a process that lasts for three nights of arduous exertion, dancing, and spirit possession, fueled by liberal doses of the mildly hallucinogenic liquor absinthe—all of which is designed to separate our sense of who we are from the raw potential of who we have been and still can be. We enter the battle to fight for reconnection with our firstborn and unbroken—that is, unconditioned—spirit and the energy of the universe around us. We remain blindfolded until we achieve this sense of our selves.

In Western religions there is something of this search for the numinous through experience with the dark. In fourteenth-century England, for example, there was a rapid flowering of the mystical and Anchorite traditions, influenced by *The Cloud of Unknowing,* an anonymously written doctrine that advocated the Dionysian practice of Divine Darkness. Anchorite men and Anchoress women aimed—through a dedicated inward spiritual life, much of it spent in dark monastic cells—to achieve more than the salvation of their souls: their divine task was to anchor the energy of transformation on Earth through interior illumination and visionary experience that would carry spiritual truth to the world.

The route to this illumination for the Anchoress Julian of Norwich (1343–1416) was darkness and isolation from the world. From her earliest youth, Julian had been called to the knowing of God and she expressed three great desires: to witness the Passion of Christ—to "taste God"—so she might have a direct experience of the divine; to fall mortally ill at the age of thirty, so she might be closer to God; and to feel the stigmata wounds of Saint Cecilia, so she could feel compassion and feel a deeper connection to the divine.

While still young she joined the Church of Saints Julian and Edward in Norwich. There she dwelt alone in a dark empty cell, entertaining remarkable God-sent visions and teachings that she recorded in her *Showings.*

Just as she had wished, Julian fell ill at the age of thirty, becoming so paralyzed that her breathing suffered and she drifted close to death. Her most profound "showing" occurred during the administration of last rites, when the head of Christ on the crucifix of a priest began to bleed from its crown of thorns. Then she was shown an object the size of a hazelnut, lying in the palm of her hand. She wondered what it was and an answer came into her mind:

> It is all that is made. . . . It lasts and always shall last because God loves it, and just in this way everything has its being.[8]

With this came the spiritual lesson that until she was "oned" to the divine in herself, she would not find lasting bliss. To accomplish this union, she wrote, we must all understand that everything created is nothing—the darkness is the light—and we all stand naked before God. This visionary showing was as healing as it was intense and her illness departed soon afterward.

For Julian, human beings did not experience oneness with God only because of their lack of faith in its possibility. She was convinced that prayer helped to overcome this failing by helping us to focus on the divine within us. With eyes closed in the darkness, our concentration flowers into a more earnest desire and we reach our soaring infinite in holy communion with our own being. Then we may realize, as Julian did in one of her showings, that:

> God is nearer to us than our own soul, for He is the ground in whom our soul stands . . . if we want to have knowing of our soul, and communion and loving with it we need to seek into our God, in whom it is enclosed
> *I it am*
> *The greatness and goodness of the Father*
> *I it am*
> *The wisdom and kindness of the Mother*
> *I it am*
> *The light and grace that is all blessed love*
> *I it am*
> *I it am, the Trinity*
> *I it am, the Oneness*

I it am, the highest goodness of all things
I it am that makes you to love
I it am that makes you to long
I it am, the endless fulfilling of all true desires[9]

In medieval lantern churches and gothic abbeys, darkness was also considered part of the architectural design of the structure itself, so that stepping into one of these places removed the individual from normal vision into a landscape of spiritual seeing, from light and the world of forms into a sacred plane where God can be sensed in shades and shadows.

The French art historian Emile Male writes of one of these cathedrals—Chartres—as a place of "somber twilight," where only thin fingers of sunlight sparkle in the gloom, high up in the clerestories.[10]

This twilight limits our vision for at least an hour after we enter, until our eyes adjust to the darkness. We can see things only dimly, their edges blurring into indistinct patterns. The small amount of light that does exist is strained through windows of cobalt blue and red glass, which allow for the least amount of visual acuity. Because clear glass was also available to the architects of Chartres, we must assume that these colors were deliberately chosen for this effect. Similarly, in the *ambulatoire* of Notre-Dame de Paris, light is filtered to such an extent that visitors can barely see their hands before their faces, even on the sunniest of days.

Within these cathedrals, everything is perceived in a "diffused, coloristic darkness" that is quite deliberate—a "darkness which is beyond Light, [where] we pray that we may come and may attain unto vision through the loss of sight and knowledge," as Dionysius puts it in his *Mystical Theology* II.[11]

By being unable to see the physical world around us, we become able to transcend conditioned reality and to know things as the way they are, beyond our normal perception and understanding. We ascend spiritually in the darkness to meet with God through the experience of a superessential darkness beyond being, which is otherwise hidden by the light of existent things or, in other words, by separated forms and opposites. In short, we can know God and return to our source only through darkness. Light merely obscures our experience beneath the facts of life.

The medieval physics and metaphysics seen in Chartres and Notre-Dame are based on Plato's theory of optics, which asserts that physical light hides God from us, but by embracing darkness, we may move to that place without form where God is waiting for us (or where we can reassemble ourselves to become God once again). This place is the void, the sea of energy, the consciousness of the universe, where all is one and there is no separation. Darkness: the place where I am That, I am Thou, and the eye of darkness sees.

Try This
◑ Awakening the Senses

Arrange before you a selection of foods, some you like and some you don't, then enter darkness by putting on a blindfold or simply closing your eyes. Next, experience each of these foods with your other senses, leaving the sense of taste for last: How do they feel? Do they have a sound as you touch their surfaces? What is their smell? Their shape? Consistency? As you explore these characteristics, you may find memories and associations arising for each one, links to an earlier time or a totally different experience. What do these mean to you?

Finally, with eyes still closed, taste each food. How has the taste of each changed now that you don't see the food itself? What information do you receive through your taste buds and other senses as to what these foods really mean to you? What is the real reason, for example, that you like or dislike them?

Shamans say that everything in the world has a spirit and this spirit offers a message for us about who we are. Now that you see these foods differently in the darkness, what is the real message from each of them and what does each say about you?

◑ The Spirit of Nature

I believe in God—only I spell it N.a.t.u.r.e.

FRANK LLOYD WRIGHT

Now that your competence with darkness is growing, take yourself to a place in nature where you can be alone and undisturbed. Put on a blindfold or close your eyes and feel the sun on your face and the earth beneath you. Chew a blade of grass. Hear the wind in the trees. Each of these has a spirit too, and the road to our communion with all of them is through quiet contemplation of our senses and the meanings they reveal.

What is nature telling you about itself, about who you are, and about the relationship between you?

◑ The Cave of Souls

Shamans take journeys to other worlds, entering them through dark places such as subterranean caves, where they meet spirit beings to receive counsel and healing. Another way of viewing this is that they take a voyage of the creative imagination into their souls or unconscious and find hidden wisdom deep within themselves.

With eyes closed, imagine yourself entering a cave that takes you down into the earth, into a darkness in which you still can see. Tunnels run from the main chamber, and at the end of each there may be information that is useful to you regarding your life, dreams, and the steps you need to take in the world. As you stand at the entrance to each tunnel, ask yourself, "What do I most need to know about myself in relation to—," finishing this query with whatever it is that you must have answered. Then step into the tunnel and explore. It may be that a guide, object, symbol, or wise spirit being of some kind will be waiting for you there with the information you seek. Accept what is offered and see how it might relate to your life.

Now imagine that a great healer appears who offers to take away your cares and concerns. What is the one most pressing problem that you would like to address? What does this healer do—or suggest you do—to heal it?

Will you do it?

3

The Mythological Mind

The Impact of Darkness on Those
Who Enter There

*The darkness is inconceivable. . . . All orientation is gone, and you
are in a darkness that never saw the sun.*

JOSEPH CAMPBELL, *REFLECTIONS ON THE ART OF LIVING*

DESPITE TODAY'S ADVANCES in the psychology of consciousness, the human experience of darkness is one area in which modern science itself remains largely in the dark.

As far as we know, there is no research into the experience of darkness, per se. We do have limited information on the psychology (or, more properly, the neuroscience) of blindness and, at the time of this writing, there is a growing interest in *nyctophobia* (fear of the dark, particularly in children), but these studies tend to focus on brain-based and biochemical responses, with the intention of effecting a cure or easing a problem. Darkness is therefore regarded as something to be "dealt with" or controlled rather than experienced, and its impact is considered to be rooted in the organic—in the physical matter of the brain, rather than in human *consciousness*.

This perception speaks to the agenda and basic concerns of modern science and medicine within our separated and specialized world: to control, change, and "cure" rather than study, learn from, and integrate. The assumption is that our experience of darkness cannot be good in itself and has nothing to teach us, which might be regarded as a rather Christianized view: that in some way darkness equals evil while light equals good or God. This is apparent in the Christian iconography that depicts hell as a dark and fiery place, while heaven shines with the light of God and the saints are illuminated by haloes.

This modern Western view of darkness is by no means universal, however. In Greek mythology, for example, when Theseus sought out the minotaur, he entered a dark labyrinth, a parable that speaks metaphorically of a need to face the darkness within ourselves in order to slay the monsters we hide in our unconscious—of an imperative to face the dark night of the soul and, through it, to find our light.

In his book *One River,* Wade Davis tells us that in contrast to this Western view, the Kogi Indians of the Sierra Nevada regard darkness as a vital tool for self-discovery and a vehicle of initiation for the elect into the priesthood of the tribe.

The Kogi are a pre-Columbian people and one of the oldest tribes of the Americas. Furthermore, they are the only tribe that was never conquered by Europeans, with their Christian notions of God and striving for the light. Of passing interest here is the fact that the Kogi, a tribe who embrace the sanctity of darkness, are a peaceful people whose members have never killed one of their own. This is in marked contrast to the Christian races who worship a God of light.

Their use and application of darkness is phenomenally ancient in origin. For the Kogi, an individual is called to the priesthood through divination that is made as soon as a child is born. If chosen, an infant is taken from his family and carried into the mountains, where he is raised by priests. "There the child lives a nocturnal life, completely shut away from the sun, forbidden even to know the light of the full moon."[1]

The child remains in darkness for up to *nineteen years.* "Because the initiates know only darkness, they acquire the gift of visions," says Davis.

"They become clairvoyant, capable of seeing not only into the future and past, but through all material illusions of the universe. In trance they can travel through the lands of the dead and into the hearts of the living."[2]

Finally, after nineteen years of living in darkness, the great day arrives when the initiate is ready to greet the world. On a clear morning, when the sun is rising over the mountains, bringing with it the transcendent dawn, the initiate is led into the light. For the first time ever he sees the beauty of a world that, to him, has existed only as an idea, a concept, a notion, before this moment. "You see," says his teacher, "it is as I told you."[3]

It is a beautiful and poetic experience that Davis describes, but does the initiate truly develop from his time in darkness the talents and skills this author relates—gifts of clairvoyance and transcendence, the ability to cut through the illusions of the world and to meet with spirits and ancestors? Modern science cannot tell us if these effects are real because its focus has been on ridding the world of darkness instead of studying its remarkable possibilities.

The historical origins of this focus lie in the attacks by the Church on such pioneering scientists as Bruno, Galileo, and Copernicus during the Renaissance and Reformation. In reaction, during the arguably misnamed Age of Enlightenment, Western science and medicine decreed that souls and spirits did not exist and were therefore not relevant to scientific study and medical practice. The perpetuation of this position into our age limits the parameters of science by decreeing a priori that certain phenomena cannot exist.

From our own experience and from the reports of participants on our Darkness Visible retreats, however, the experience of the Kogi initiate can actually be reproduced even in a quite limited time frame and within a modern context. A mountain hermitage or labyrinthine cave is not needed.

Shamanically speaking, there is good reason for this: we live at a time when the veils are thin, and relative to the time required just a generation or two ago, people are therefore able to attain threshold experiences and encounters with the transcendental in the briefest of periods.

We no longer have the luxury of long periods of time for the exploration of our interior landscapes. This thinning between visible and invisible realms has occurred, in part, because of what is commonly perceived as the spiritual emergency that is upon us—a time in which vast numbers of people live increasingly dispirited lives, their souls having become hollowed out by the spiritually barren landscape they traverse. As we have repeatedly witnessed, in darkness there is a way of seeing without the eyes and a way of communicating beyond and without words all that needs to be seen and heard in order to assure the swift dispersal of the darkest clouds on the horizon of the self and, in doing so, to heal the splits that divide the outer world.

We also, of course, benefit from our ancestors' pioneering work in darkness. We do not have to reinvent darkness work, but instead have only to learn from our forebears and apply their methodologies for tracking the interior world. Because of this, our communion with the spirits of the dark is more quickly facilitated—that is, in hours instead of years.

At the outset of our Darkness Visible retreats, participants are ceremonially initiated, one by one, into the dark realms. After stepping forward into an area that has been blessed and awakened, each is ritually cleansed using herbs and resins that burn within a bee smoker, a traditional cleansing tool from the shamanic Path of Pollen. Other forms of healing and cleansing may also take place in order to ready the participant and shift his or her consciousness to a calmer and more receptive state.

Participants are then asked individually to state their prayers and intentions for the experience they are about to engage in. On the shorter retreats we facilitate, participants cover their eyes with a Mindfold,* a flexible, black plastic faceplate backed with high-density soft-foam padding that fits snugly to the face. Its internal cutouts allow the user to experience total darkness with eyes open, thus creating an ongoing environment to encourage the shamanic art of seeing in the dark.

---

* The Mindfold, originally designed by the artist Alex Grey (see *Transfigurations,* published by Inner Traditions, for the flavor of his work), is manufactured by Mindfold Inc., 8043 East 7th Street, Tucson, AZ 85710. Web site: www.mindfold.com. E-mail: info@mindfold.com. Telephone: 520-885-3700, 888-705-3805. Fax: 520-885-1846.

Once the Mindfold is fitted, participants are led back to their seats, where they settle into the infinite black void that now surrounds them, and the room itself is darkened. Each voyager into darkness, along with typically twenty-nine other participants, will remain in this state for a minimum of five days and nights, with more advanced retreats lasting from thirteen to twenty-three days.

To give you an idea of the psychological impact of darkness, we include below the comments and assessment of one of these participants, Kevin, which address his emotional, physical, mental, and transcendent/spiritual experiences during his five-day retreat.

A PASSAGE INTO DARKNESS

When darkness is viewed as a metaphor, there is often fear behind it, expressed or unexpressed, that it will be painful, blinding, and negative. "When a man wends his way down into the secret heart of darkness he finds shadowy figures with burning eyes that seem to accuse him of monstrous crimes and terrible failures," as Sam Keen writes in his book, *Fire in the Belly*.

But this is often a cultural expectation of what hides in the dark. In reality, those who wend their way along these labyrinths of the secret heart often find liberation, luminosity, and healing, as the following account shows.

Kevin is a forty-five-year-old man from Ireland who works as a therapist, though he is also trained in graphic design.

He explains why he was drawn to the Darkness Visible retreat:

> About fifteen years ago I was giving a public lecture on behalf of the C. G. Jung Institute of Ireland, and during the question and answer session afterwards, the subject arose of the increasing alienation of individuals within modern society. I opined that this was reflected in our paucity of communal initiatory rituals, apart

from those which have become debased, empty, or secularized. The question was then asked: "What true communal initiations are available today?"

This question has stayed with me down through the years. I saw Darkness Visible as an initiation, of which I was much in need.

Kevin also acknowledges an element of personal healing in the work: "It was well beyond my comfort zone, as I would dread to lose my sight. I wanted to deepen my 'seeing'; I wanted to be 'hollowed out.' My childhood visions and trials also took place mainly in darkness."

What follows is Kevin's experience of darkness, which seems to have much in common with that of the Kogi initiate, including visions, distortions of time, the ability to travel into the future and past, the awareness of the closeness of spirit, and the passing on of information from the world of nonordinary reality.

It seems remarkable that much of the nineteen-year experience of the Kogi priest-to-be can be compressed into a short five-day framework. We can only imagine how much deeper—and how much more worthy of study—must be the experience of the Kogi.

Preparing for the Dark World

At the beginning of the Darkness Visible retreat, participants sit in a circle and prepare to enter darkness through the ritual application of the Mindfolds.

As we sat in circle before entering the dark, I had the impression of us being the psychic or spiritual equivalent of test pilots or astronauts about to rocket off into the unknown. The impression was reinforced by the space-age look of the Mindfold, which glinted on some of our foreheads like the high-tech visors of astronauts preparing to head for inner space. It made me relax and smile, and I realized I was in very special company. The support of my companions made it all seem less crazy than my ego was telling me this was.

I was afraid I'd overreached myself in taking on this challenge.

I doubted myself, my willpower, while at the same time recognizing that any initiation worth its salt should provoke such doubts and fears. Then, just as we began to enter darkness, I surrendered and slipped into a dreamy, calming inevitability.

The Initiation into Darkness

The experience of people's entrance into darkness can be powerful and emotional for both those experiencing this new state and those nearby who are observing or otherwise sharing in their departure.

> I cried on and off during people's entrance into darkness—tears of joy and empathy with [their] fear and trepidation. It was so beautiful to see.
>
> I felt a sense of community very strongly, a bond of deep affection and pride in their courage being forged with my companions. The trust we showed in opening to our fears was very beautiful. As each person entered, each death/birth into the dark had its own distinct characteristics, and I was able to sense this when I was sighted and after I entered myself.

Feelings upon entering darkness can be varied. It is not unusual for participants to experience a range of emotions as they step forward into this new territory and experience specific aspects of the ritual, such as the use of smoking incense.

> At first, I thought wild horses would have to drag me kicking and screaming into the dark, but it was a tribute to the initiation process that I felt a powerful *knowing* at one stage that my time had come and could not be denied.
>
> I felt both humbled and proud, as I stepped forward, that I was keeping my appointment with spirit. I was still nervous and jittery and wondering when I'd get an irresistible urge to rip off the Mindfold—would I last five minutes or an hour? But when I

felt the incense pour over me from the [bee smokers], I felt a deep calm and I felt myself truly falling into the dark.

My prayer standing on the threshold of the dark was that I would be "hollowed out" so that I could displace my ego more easily. Also, that I would be able to "see" a lot better, and that I would be able to live more fully in a state of love.

As I entered, again I felt afraid and I spoke with my spirits. They burst upon me in riotous disorder, all at once, laughing and slapping me on the back. The big joke, apparently, was that they'd been there all along, waiting for me to arrive.

Visions and Dreams

My memories of Darkness Visible now are, ironically, of all the wonderful things I've seen! I was blessed by the most incredibly beautiful and awe-inspiring visions—by turns ridiculous, frightening, tearful, self-affirming, awesome, and joyous—everything, in fact, an initiation should be.

The arrival of visions often marks the darkness experience from the very outset. These visions may include images of animal spirits, ancestors, galaxies and stars, or any other sensory connections drawn from deep within the self. Already the mind is in contact with a greater sense of reality beyond everyday concerns and, indeed, beyond the here and now. Some participants report a sense of physically traveling out of their bodies, for example, and away from this time and space, into a spirit world or a mythic landscape among the stars. Simultaneous with this initial shift comes a questioning of what is real. Is "reality" the body that sits in darkness in this room—or the mind that travels to the far-most corners of the universe and meets the beings who occupy this space?

The feeling—to borrow a phrase from Terence McKenna—is one of "true hallucinations"; a sense that these images and visions are real and unreal at the same time, and the realization that the line between the two is very thin, since imagining them at all will make them real.

Almost immediately [after] I put on the Mindfold, I began to have visions. It began as soon as I was smudged with one of the bee-keeper puffers. Part of me was aware of what was being used, but immediately [when] I heard it, it sounded exactly like a huge dog huffing in front of me and I was before the guardian of the spirit world. As soon as he (or I) passed, the visions began.

A smoky white mist formed, and the tendrils of this mist formed images—objects, parts of buildings, geometric shapes, fantastic and grotesque creatures, beautiful faces, rolling balls of flame, storm-tossed waves, lots of abstract patterns like sound waves in sand or snow or ash, and so on. Some of the most fascinating were pictographs formed in white lines, and I realized where those so-called aboriginal images on rocks had come from.

Each image formed in a 3-D darkness, revolving, resolving, dissolving, or passing from my view. This continued virtually throughout the entire retreat to a greater or lesser degree. It was most intense as I lay in bed and was unoccupied with other tasks. It was absolutely fascinating, like being in the front row of a cosmic cinema.

I deliberately withheld (as much as possible) any intellectual analysis or questioning of these images, content merely that they had visited me. The vast majority, while very real and immediate, had a pallor about them, a lack of color (but not of vitality), often just being shades of gray.

I trained and worked as a graphic artist for several years, but I'm at a loss in trying to visually depict some of the amazing spirits I met.

Years ago, one of my teachers told me how his father stepped out behind his cottage one night to relieve himself. There was a stream behind his cottage and a small stone bridge spanned it. It was known as a fairy bridge but no one in the locality could recall the reason why. This elderly man was a musician of traditional Irish music (he played fiddle). As he was relieving himself, he heard the most beautiful fiddle music he'd ever heard coming from the bridge. He stood there and listened to the entire melody, a melody so sweet, my teacher said, it made him weep. He'd been playing music all his life and had never heard such a tune.

When it finished he went back inside to try to copy it on the fiddle. Traditional musicians play and learn by ear, and often with just one hearing of a tune they can replicate it in its entirety. My teacher's father, even though he'd been playing fiddle for over forty years, couldn't remember any of what he'd heard well enough to play it, and was left only with the memory of its beauty.

I'm beginning to understand some of what that old man must have felt.

I found that my dreams and visions sometimes presaged the scheduled work. For instance, the night before we did work traveling forward in time to meet our future selves [one of the practices undertaken during the workshop], I dreamed I was in a class learning healing techniques and that I was in charge of the time machine we would be using (it resembled a large boxlike antique camera).

But it wasn't simply that what I saw was so profound. It seemed encoded, so to speak, with a sense of peace, of absolute clarity, of being beyond or between time, and with quietude—the intangible yet intensely present elements that permeate a visit from the sacred. I feel that it was these nonvisual components which carried much of the information I needed to receive. This is what made it more real and more personally relevant than a mere image in ordinary reality. I suppose in Jungian terms I'm talking of numinosity, the quality that accompanies an archetypal encounter.

I saw several things during the shamanic healing session [another workshop practice], but the most stunning is something I'll remember for the rest of my life: I felt raw power blasting over me, which then became a rolling sea of flame. As I looked closer I could see coils of flame forming a wall. Then it drew back and I could see that each flame was in fact a feather in a giant wing. At this realization, it pulled back further and an absolutely enormous bird composed of fire flew over me with such a feeling of majesty and power that I was left gasping. It was so, so beautiful. What an incredible extravagance this world is!

Effects of Storytelling and Poetry

Storytelling, poetry, and music play a part in Darkness Visible retreats, the pieces chosen specifically to awaken the senses and emotions and guide participants into new mythic landscapes, expanding their awareness of other possible realities revealed within the muse.

> The stories and poetry readings moved me deeply, and I was initially frustrated in not being able to immediately write them down, having to wait until I could access my diary at night. This, however, had the added bonus of ensuring I focused upon them more intently.
>
> Because of my more vulnerable state, I was affected very deeply in different ways; at times I cried or laughed or felt longings I can't intellectualize. I was aware of how important the timing was for these stories, as they seemed particularly appropriate after certain exercises or a certain day's experience. Like the music, I heard these stories and poems not with my physical ears alone, but with my body and heart.
>
> The lyrics, as well as the music, were in tune with (and sometime even crucial to) my state of mind and spirit, and I wept and laughed and listened as they entered me. I wasn't listening to music; music was playing me, resonating within me in ways I haven't felt for many years.

The Emotional Impact of Darkness

The darkness experience produces many complex emotions for those who engage it, especially for the first time. During the retreat, these may include specific feelings toward those fellow participants who, though experiencing their own transformations, are also sharing this adventure with one another.

> Emotionally, I felt free and open, as my persona dropped away. I was aware of the disintegration of social/physical boundaries. It was comforting and very touching (pun intended!) to feel the gentle weight of someone's hand on my shoulder or to feel someone brush my back or even to have someone lightly squeeze my hand as I made my way in darkness—a genderless, warm, loving contact between the bodies of kindred spirits; a lesson in how we need to touch others, heart-deep and skin-deep.
>
> There was a lovely group bonding, unhindered and uncomplicated by the visual cues which normally carry our societal and sexual prejudices. I felt very close to my companions while at the same time detached from them. This paradox was one of many I experienced, and I feel that darkness brings us close to the paradoxical nature of life.
>
> I particularly enjoyed the male bonding as it was so atypical of modern Western society. In our sleeping room there was a beautiful tenderness and strength, often soundless, which arose among us; a kind of tribal or clanlike manhood which nourished us. Chants rose among us, drumming, rattling, sighs, songs, and stories, all the antithesis of stereotypical "macho" maleness and much more powerful.
>
> My emotions felt heightened as I experienced an intensified gamut of emotions within a short space of time, some of which I haven't felt in a long time. The only emotional response I can't recall is anger, although frustration was there in abundance, especially in the early stages as I tried to adjust to my new environment.

Not all of the emotions experienced are positive ones. Darkness Visible retreats allow for meeting head-on some more difficult feelings that we do not always allow ourselves to acknowledge.

It's been a long time since I felt panic or despair. These visited me one night when there was no one around and I had become lost on the stairwell. I wandered up and down, coming to a dead end each time. How it's possible to come to a dead end on either end of a stairs I don't know, but somehow I managed it in style!

I did this for what seemed like ages, panic rising all the time. I was trapped and no one would find me—ever! We were in silence at the time, and at one point I felt someone brushing past but I couldn't ask them for help without compromising their silence also. "I'm lost," I moaned in the dark. "I'm totally and utterly lost. I haven't a clue where I am." I felt totally alone and helpless, a frightened child.

While in another reality I was quite safe and standing on a staircase only a few yards from my bedroom door, in that emotional reality I was hopelessly lost and alone in a strange, lightless land. I think of that experience sometimes in relation to my two-year-old daughter, or when I'm treating a child in my clinic. It helps me empathize more fully with their fears, which to an adult may seem trivial, but which to them are life-and-death issues.

Vulnerability is the word I would use to characterize my emotional state. The descent into darkness really did bring me closer to love, and that validates this type of work in a way that for me is totally beyond refute.

As a result of this vulnerability—resulting in permeability, the blurring of my boundaries—the course material seemed designed specifically for me. The songs I heard seemed to be written for me, or with me in mind. The stories were directed specifically at me. The exercises dovetailed with my present and past life experience.

In this dark world I felt strangely detached from other people's voyages. I was aware of their pain—I heard lots of weeping and anger, and some shouted their pain and confusion—but none of it disturbed me in the slightest and I felt absolutely no need to interfere, to make things better, other than to offer a prayer to protect my fellow travelers, whom I did indeed love.

Physical Effects

It is not just our relationship with our mental and emotional selves that changes in darkness; our bodies also react differently. It is interesting to note how physical tiredness can also result as we are forced to reinterpret the world and renegotiate our material space, unlearning patterns of behavior and actions that we have unthinkingly repeated for years. Our socialization has been deep: even our muscles carry beliefs about the world and direct our bodies in a particular way. In darkness, all of that must change. In this respect, the words of Jez, a poet who joined us as a participant on a 2005 workshop, are also interesting:

> By the second day, I felt as if my body had dissolved and melted into the air around me [which, of course, is true; at an atomic level we do blend with the environment around us, our bodies having no solid boundary], like I was floating in a warm bath of air. The only things that remained were my hands. These became my eyes and my fingertips became extremely sensitive, as if I was really seeing with them. Apart from them, my body ceased to exist.
>
> I found the course very taxing in that I needed to be constantly aware of where I was and of my spatial relationships in ordinary reality. I needed to hold onto information that I would normally have discarded as superfluous: how many steps were in each flight of stairs, where the bathrooms were, the judgments and adjustments needed to pour a glass of water, and so on. I tend to view the brain as primarily a filtering system, and I had to learn to adjust that filter so that a lot of what was previously discarded was now retained and vice versa.
>
> I've never had to maintain focus on mundane reality for such a long period while at the same time opening myself up to the

nonordinary world. Keeping a mental foothold in both worlds simultaneously was both tiring and exhilarating.

I was surprised [at] how physically tired I was and how grateful I was to be able to lie down. Initially I was fearful of hurting myself by bumping into things, but as time went on, I relaxed more and gained some confidence in moving around, although I never quite got to the stage where I could skip gaily down a corridor.

Once or twice I actually felt my own physical body distort. At first I thought my Mindfold had slipped at an angle, even though no light was coming through, but then I realized that it was as though my left eye had dropped several inches and my skin had become rubbery. Also at times I felt as if I were wearing a heavy hood (I remember checking if someone had draped something over my head) or as if hands were being held over me or being laid upon my shoulders. It was a comforting feeling and sustained me at times when I felt overwhelmed, lonely, or fearful. It reminded me of the hooded initiates of the ancient world and the blessing the ancients used to give: "May the gods hold their hands over you."

For the first time in my conscious memory, touch and hearing became my primary senses to ensure my physical safety, and I became grateful to my fingers, my hands, arms, legs, for keeping me safe and guiding me. I enjoyed being able to focus on tasting my food, as, lacking eye contact, I didn't have the same distractions and could avoid social interaction to concentrate on a particularly tasty mouthful. Not being able to see the food meant my eyes didn't presuppose or impose a taste upon my taste buds, and the experience was intensified.

My hearing was also intensified, and I could identify sound direction more accurately than when sighted. More important, however, was the sensation of sounds going through me and resonating inside me, rather than a superficial hearing with external ears. This was particularly true when I absorbed the stories and music. I felt I was listening with my body rather than just with my ears. I can still hear those sounds inside me when I now enter darkness.

The most fascinating and wonderful sensation was of the earth beneath my feet and all around me. At times, as I walked, I could "see" and feel myself by turns sinking into or rising from the ground, or walking through slight undulations in the ground, like a ghost in the land. Once I was wading through a sea, even though I knew I was walking on grass in ordinary reality. At first I would wave my hands before me, expecting to feel the hillock, or wall, or tree I was absolutely convinced was before me, and be amazed to feel nothing. Eventually I just relaxed and enjoyed the sensation of experiencing one landscape while maintaining an awareness of my bearings in the other landscape of ordinary reality.

REACQUAINTING OURSELVES WITH GOD: ENCOUNTERS WITH THE NUMINOUS

Within the formal structure of the Darkness Visible retreat, various exercises and practices are either carried out by participants in darkness or carried out around them by the facilitators in order to deepen the participants' experiences. The latter include events ranging from explorations of music, poetry, and storytelling—which, when we're sighted, receive limited attention from us relative to their mood and composition but which, in darkness, we can hear in full to a profound emotional or even spiritual effect—to a group healing session during which participants are invited to call in their spirit healers so that facilitators, using shamanic methods, can conduct a healing for the purposeful integration of the self. But in darkness even the simple act of eating takes on a newfound profundity by allowing the taste buds to experience without prejudice what is laid before the hungry explorer.

Other exercises include a "temple dreaming" in which the spirit of Asklepios, the ancient healer of the Greeks, is invoked as part of a visualization experience for healing (see pages 130–32); a shamanic journey to the ancestors to heal the wounds of the past (see pages 121–23); and, finally, a commitment at a crossroads on the final day, during which participants are invited to step forward into a new future, to remain where they are at the present, or to step back into the person they were before their darkness began (see pages 147–49). This final exercise precedes their ritual unveiling and return to the world of sight. Typically, a very new world awaits.

These exercises and their effects are dealt with in more detail in later chapters, where we include the responses and thoughts of Kevin and other participants. Most can be tried by readers who wish to experience the phenomena of the work.

Final Reflections

After finishing the retreat and returning to their everyday lives, participants face the challenge of integrating their new awarenesses from darkness experience into jobs, home lives, and relationships. In many instances the greatest effects of time spent in darkness are not fully realized until this integration begins, as Kevin's words suggest:

> My dreams [during darkness] were very vivid and full of personal instruction. Sometimes a dream the night before would be [clairvoyantly] relevant to the next day's work.
>
> [But] there's no point, of course, in having all these wonderful experiences unless they lead to [my] living life more deeply and fully. I've noticed changes: a quiet sense of feeling more balanced and at peace.
>
> At work, one of my clients who suffers from a chronic and debilitating neurological disease asked me how I'd got on at the workshop. I left aside the more esoteric aspects and told her about the physical and emotional difficulties involved. I told her of the frustration of having to slow myself right down; having trivial distances take on marathon proportions; having to be dependent on others for the simplest tasks; having to weigh in my mind if it was

worth the enormous effort to go up and down stairs, to eat, or go to the toilet; how each step carried uncertainty and every corridor was an expedition into the unknown; how I had to be aware of exactly where I was in order to be able to get around. I spoke of the tiredness I felt as my body tried to adjust with my new internal and external environment.

As I spoke, she was nodding in agreement and her smile of satisfaction grew wider. "Well," she said, when I'd finished, "now you have some idea of what life has been like for me for the last twenty years!" That certainly put things in perspective.

The overall change has been an increased awareness of the love that binds the universe. This awareness feels like that protected feeling we get as children when we crawl up onto our parents' laps for a hug or a little sleep.

Having been in darkness, I trust more in love, and consequently my behavior as a parent, a healer, a human being is, I think, more real and confident [and] also unrelated to the size of my ego—[I feel] a deeper empathy for those around me. My clinical practice has benefited enormously.

My teacher once told me that the type of healing/medical practice I will have will be a mirror of what is going on inside me, and to therefore watch for changes in my clinic (the type of people coming in and the ailments they present), as they will reflect changes deep within myself.

On my return [one] client (with no knowledge of this retreat) told me that she had finally come to face the trauma that had haunted her all her life. "My healing lies in the heart of darkness and I have to enter into it to find it. Does that make any sense to you?" she asked.

Darkness Visible was a validation of my faith in myself and my faith in my gods and goddesses. It was awe-inspiring to see beneath the visual surface of things, to see energy in its primal state and to then communicate with the archetypal forms it takes.

More than all of this, though, was my beautiful vision of the world when I returned from the dark: of Pan riding every photon and of love permeating every molecule of this beautiful, incredible world.

TRY THIS

◖ Initiation into Darkness

As we mentioned, while participants in our retreats step forward into darkness, they are asked to make their prayers, though no prescription or restriction is given as to what these prayers might be. The entire process of initiation into darkness may take several hours, depending on the group size, so people have a good deal of time to focus on what they really want and wish to pray for.

Imagine yourself preparing to step forward into darkness. Close your eyes and allow yourself to dream what your prayers might be. Give yourself as long as it takes until they are clear to you: What is it that you truly want? Without misleading yourself, try to determine why you don't have it yet. When you are ready, state your prayers out loud.

◖ Hearing the Truth

When we are in darkness, sounds and words register very differently than they do in the world of light. Our barriers fall away as visual cues recede, and our prejudices and reliance on stereotypes—usually based on appearances—begin to fade. Instead, we connect with a more emotionally whole response and we start to hear not only what is said (or not said), but the real meaning behind the words. Emotions open up in the dark and we connect with others from a different space.

With your eyes closed, try listening to a favorite piece of music or perhaps the words of a friend. Or record yourself speaking aloud and wholeheartedly about something that means something to you. Then play it back to yourself and, with your eyes closed, hear what you really have to say.

What greater depths of meaning can you touch and what new emotions do you feel?

◑ Future-Seeing

As Kevin also remarks, some of the deep states that we enter in darkness can even have a precognitive quality. This is not unique to Darkness Visible. Many spiritual traditions hold that, when we truly still our minds by entering silence and darkness and focus instead on our breath and relaxing ourselves so that we enter a state of flow (see chapter 4), we bring our minds in tune with a much vaster consciousness that is either within us (the world of active imagination) or outside of us (a place of sentient energy that some Eastern traditions call the Void). These traditions suggest that, at some deep level, we are all energetically linked; all of us aspects of God from a time before separation. Why, then, should we not know one another's minds or sense what the future holds? Surely, such things are not beyond the capability of God.

Try closing your eyes and allowing yourself to deeply enter into darkness. Being as still and as quiet as you can, hold an intention to see the future, to see, perhaps, an incident that has yet to happen but is practical, real, and obvious, so that you will know it when it happens. Then simply relax into whatever images emerge and explore them as they occur.

During ordinary consciousness throughout the next few days, remain as alert as you can to see if these images actually come to be. If they do, what does this say about what you have within you and all that you might be?

4

The Landscape of Myth and Emotion

The Psychology of Darkness

There can be no transforming of darkness into light and of apathy into movement without emotion.

C. G. JUNG, *THE UNDISCOVERED SELF*

WHAT WE KNOW from both our experience of being human and the spiritual studies available to us is that there is a greater life than the one we habitually lead (or that leads us). Our shamans, poets, artists, and seers, the great mythologists of our cultures, have always known that beneath the veneer of our socially conditioned reality there beats a heart of darkness, a vast and magical mystery that we can never really know.

Houngan Andre Pierre, a shaman-priest of Haitian Vodou, puts this succinctly and beautifully:

> The real world is created by magic.
>
> The first magician is God, who created people with his own hands from the dust of the Earth. People originated by magic in all countries of the world.
>
> No one lives of the flesh. Everyone lives of the spirit.[1]

Interestingly, modern science now endorses the presence of this mystery. Our scientists tell us, for example, that the brain is a vast and intricate organ, but that we use barely 5 percent of its capacity during our normal waking states and are conscious of only 5 percent of our brain's cognitive activity, while the remaining 95 percent remains unknown—a mystery, a potential, an uncharted territory. As Marianne Szegedy-Maszak states in the title of her article at US News.com, "Your Unconscious Makes 95 Percent of Your Decisions."[2]

Szegedy-Maszak also quotes Paul Whelan, a neuroscientist at the University of Wisconsin, who says that "most of what we do every minute of every day is unconscious." We rely instead on what is called the *adaptive unconscious,* a sort of interface between the 5 percent of our brain that acts mainly from habit and the vast pool of unconscious power within us. At its most mundane level, the adaptive unconscious is that liminal state that "makes it possible for us to, say, turn a corner in our car without having to go through elaborate calculations to determine the precise angle of the turn, the velocity of the automobile, the steering radius of the car," and so on, but that may be capable of much, much more.

Gerald Zaltman, professor emeritus at Harvard Business School, has been studying the adaptive mind and finds that its potential goes far beyond the habitual. According to Zaltman, the adaptive unconscious is mythological and metaphorical in nature, responding to interior images and symbols rather than to rational thought. Participants in his studies are asked to cut out pictures that represent their feelings about a particular subject, even if they don't know why. When they do so, they often discover "a core, a deep metaphor simultaneously embedded in a unique setting"[3] and are drawn to heroic myths, universal images such as blood and fire, or deep concepts such as that of journey and transformation.

These metaphors are not at all esoteric, but instead have very practical applications. Zaltman, for instance, has used them to help an architectural firm design a children's hospital with the intention of making a frightening stay more bearable. Children were asked to cut out pictures they associated with hospitals and were then interviewed to explore the thoughts, feelings, and associations triggered by these images. A stream of metaphors emerged, with one child bringing in a picture of a sad-looking dog, for example, "because that's the way I feel when I'm in the ICU [intensive care unit]."

Each picture was then scanned and added to a collage that sparked further discussions and interviews from which even deeper themes emerged, including key metaphors centering on transformation, control, connection, and energy.

Translating this into physical space means that the hospital, when it opens in 2008, will be decorated with images of butterflies, a major and universal symbol of transformation. Rooms will be more homey and less institutional and patients will have more control over their personal space. There will also be a large garden, visible from all rooms, signifying energy, transformation, and growth.

The work of Zaltman and others resonates with us because it reminds us of how the mind really wants to work: not with date planners, diaries, mathematical formulas, legal procedures, and adherence to rules and regulations, but in response to the richness of metaphor and symbols. Because of this, it often finds itself at odds with the modern world, which has forgotten the magic within us, the mystery of which we are a part, and, in Andre Pierre's words, the presence of God within us.

SPIRIT IN THE RATIONAL WORLD

In scientific terms, the brain is separated into two distinct spheres, like a large walnut, and connected by a bridge of nerves called the *corpus callosum*. Each sphere has a completely different function: one is in charge of rational, standard, operational functions; the other half, barely used in the modern world, is involved with states of intuition, dreaming, and visionary experience.

It is the rational sphere that is most empowered in daily living and is the side of ourselves that we are most often taught to use—in schools, for example, in the mathematical and mechanical subjects we are required to learn, as well as in the rational approach to learning itself that is imposed on us, in which even poetry, the music of the soul, is reduced to the measurement of stanzas, iambic pentameter, and intellectual analyses of the poet's intentions (as if these can be known). Additionally, in schools there is a hidden curriculum that teaches us to habitually follow rules and procedures—to salute the flag, stay at our desks, respond to the bell. This feeds the rational mind, which thrives on order rather than creativity, and prepares us for the world of work and a life in which we will be further initiated into the rules of our linear world.

In fact, the basic constructs of our lives, from our earliest to our latest experiences of ordinary reality, have been built to support the rational mind, and our intuitive selves, as a consequence, have atrophied. These rational constructs for living are, by and large, given to us visually—in a teacher's words on the blackboard, where we may first learn the alphabet and so define the limits of our language and our world; in the learned critique read from a book; in the images on a television screen bringing us news of "how it is" in our world.

All of these images are instructions in how to be "normal," how to fit in to society instead of exploring the dreaming landscapes of our creative intuition, where all things may be possible, limited only by what we choose to see there.

We can enter this dreaming world only with our eyes closed, in reveries and flights of fancy. It is a world that offers us expansion instead of contraction, a place for which our society feels mostly morbid fear. The act of living, once again, has become one of separation from ourselves and our full potential as we learn to be socialized beings operating with 5 percent of our brain capacity, instead of becoming dreamers and visionaries in full enjoyment of our potential.

Against this backdrop, it is perhaps not surprising that we as a society have conducted so little research into darkness, the channel through which we may reach our infinite selves. Our rational minds simply have not thought of studying it; nor has our society provided funding for such study.

This leaves us at some disadvantage in terms of this book, of course, in that there is hardly any published material for us to refer to when trying to explain the visionary effects of darkness. We can turn only to the research that we ourselves have done (and which you can add to right now, of course, by simply closing your eyes).

We can, however, consider certain aspects of the darkness experience that can be found in the psychological literature: in darkness there is a sense of isolation and distancing of ourselves from the outside world. We have only to close our eyes to have the sense, almost immediately, of an almost physical barrier between ourselves and the ordinary world. If we keep our eyes closed for a while, we may also begin to experience the arrival of images as the outside world fades away and we become part of a more mythological inner landscape.

We may then sense a curious slowing down of the world—as if time itself has ceased to be—as our journey inward continues. Finally, perhaps, there comes a sense of calm, a peaceful relaxation combined with a great interest in this new world of inner being that we may never before have explored.

All of these elements of experience await us in darkness, and we do have studies that can guide our understanding in these areas: the research conducted on meditation, for example (the deliberate slowing down of the mind, which tends to occur naturally in darkness); the experiences of the mind when the body is isolated from the external world or exists in states of sensory deprivation; and the research into the mental imagery that may be stimulated during altered states of consciousness.

It is to these that we now turn to understand the creative potential of darkness and how it might give us access to more of our selves and the worlds within us beyond the 5 percent of brain power and capacity that we habitually use.

THE MEDITATIVE MIND

What I give form to in daylight is only 1 percent of what
I have seen in darkness.

M. C. ESCHER

In the *American Journal of Psychotherapy,* M. DelMonte writes that a central aspect of meditation is its "constriction"[4]—that is, during meditation, with our eyes closed, the mind is constricted in that a reduced number of external experiences are presented to it. We have much less sensory input available to us from the world, and in any case, by the very nature of the experience, we do not focus on the meaning of this input, but rather on an experience beyond knowing that is characterized by the cessation of mental processes.

For the meditator, the past, present, and future all consist of one experience: the experience itself. This is in radical contrast to the normal expectations of social living, in which habitual responses requiring little use of brain power are determined by accessing cues to behavior based on known events and likely outcomes from familiar actions. We are always thinking ahead, reflecting on the past, weighing options, assessing environmental risks, and so on—in other words, not being present here and now with the experience of living.

During meditation, however, we are focused precisely on experience itself and, because our awareness is not being channeled into a behavioral pattern, we are able to access more of our mind's potential—more of that 95 percent that conventionally remains unused.

In darkness, we see the same effects. One of our retreat participants, Alison, explains it this way:

My feelings became much more multisensorial. [Darkness] negated [many] of the "normal" cues for relating to others—that is, how people look, facial expressions and body language, and so on. The experience necessitated a reliance on other, more subtle energetic emanations—the "voice within the voice."

Darkness does not seem the place of the rational intellectual self, but much more that of the primal and intuitive. I did, at times, find myself trying to make sense of images or attach meaning to things, but somehow I found less of an urgency to do so and began to surrender to the bliss of not having to try. . . . A wave of information caressed my being, to be experienced—without analysis.

Another participant recounts very similar realizations:

My mental side shut down and took a holiday, as thoughts were pushed to the background in favor of all the other delights I was experiencing. How I perceived things changed in darkness. I felt freed to experience [my] emotions without judgment and was able to let silent tears flow [that] I would usually block or cover up. My spiritual self made itself visible and I felt a sense of the sacred and the potential within me. The inner landscapes and experiences were amazing and fantastic. I had wonderful visions of being cleansed and healed. I felt parts of me bursting open into light, connected to the universe.

Another puts it very simply when he remarks: "Your thinking mind shuts down and your visioning mind watches the action—which was plentiful. The world was more alive than it normally feels."

DelMonte suggests that reduced sensory input leads to a *hypnagogic* state—the state of drowsiness preceding sleep—which gives the mind an opportunity to explore and express otherwise repressed material. Because the part of the mind that is normally repressed in social life is the creative and intuitive self, the material that is likely to emerge in a reduced sensory state will therefore be of an emotional and nonrational nature. Because this is also accompanied by a cessation of the rational mind, we are less likely to create attachments to, or judgments of, this emerging material, and so we are able to experience it fully and in all of its richness.

Thus "silent tears" may flow, but they do not bring with them pain. Rather, the experience becomes one of the "choiceless awareness" of mental images and emotional processes that bubble up from the unconscious or mythological mind to become part of a wonderland and adventure to explore and join. Habitual responses, prejudices, and biases are abandoned and a purer and more holistic perception of reality begins to emerge.

Marius, a participant on one of our 2003 retreats, says:

> I felt my emotional body doing an all-out workout, "stretching its muscles" and letting old pains and joys come out and be fully experienced, not suppressed or hidden. Darkness helped quiet the chattering mind, for I had to concentrate on where I was and what I was doing and the more I focused on my surroundings the less the inner dialogue became. I found peace from my own inner wars.

The same point is made by others:

> A lot of what went through my mind was not much (for a change!).

> [It was] a glorious disengagement from the chatter, a slowing and expansion into the space between the spaces . . . a delicious time out of time—exploring, flowing, disengaging, and engaging. . . . [It was an] exquisite connection with spirit, self, and other.

One participant, Cedric, describes his inner experience as a "mental holiday."

> No visual incoming data to analyze, no body language, no gestures, looks, glances, "meaningful" stares . . . I realize now that I judge people visually, and within 50 feet of approaching somebody, I would

have decided whether to accept or reject any further rapport with that person. While in darkness, I met all sorts of interesting people whom I now realize I would have bypassed had I been sighted!

Such a perception of reality beyond the mind chatter and social convention is also in keeping with DelMonte's findings that meditation invokes "a nonverbal experience with an absence of thought"—that is, a movement from "cognitive-verbal" mental processes (judgments, in other words) to an emotional and preverbal response (openness and acceptance). Cedric's observations about the judgments we normally make of others are especially interesting in this regard and correspond to recent findings in psychology, which show that "how we instantly size up people has little to do with logic and a lot to do with looks. . . . Even as you're assessing the factual cues of their bodies—gender, skin color, height, age—you already seem to know whom you perceive as likable and whom you should avoid. . . . To make such social perceptions, we rely on patterns and stereotypes that we have learned throughout our lives. . . . We pull out dozens of labels from our heads and apply them to other people."[5]

Other research has shown that this sizing up happens very quickly indeed (in around 200 milliseconds) and is felt first in the emotional rather than the rational centers of the brain; indeed, "the limbic system responds to extreme sights before the sensory information perceived by the eyes even reaches the visual cortex."[6] Being in darkness is a great leveler, therefore. It cuts through our prejudices and learned responses and allows us to connect with others at a more human and humane level, freeing us from ourselves so we are available to new contacts and experiences not driven by fear and appearances.

The descent into the unsocialized mind may also be accompanied by a feeling of transcendence—equivalent to a blissful oneness with a deeper, energetic level of reality—that takes us far beyond the constructs and constrictions of the mind. When we begin to access the fullness of ourselves it may even be cosmic in scope:

I saw glowing lights flying down glowing corridors, hanging in profound space as though I was a planet in the all-silent universe seeing the gentle pinpricks of glowing stars light years away—literally out of this world.

In the darkness I met . . . patterns of cohesive disorder. It was a wonderment to see this energy display itself . . . bright, luminescent, brilliant, and formed of pure light.

[This energy] looks like bright, tiny worm shapes, wriggling and darting all around in a mad confusion that somehow forms an overall cohesive pattern that permeates the world.

According to psychologists, we comprise constructs of ourselves that teach us how to relate to the world: when we are born, we are bundles of raw potential, our minds unfettered and free, and we have the potential to become anyone we want to be; but through socialization and "lessons" about what this world is really like and the capabilities and limitations within us, we begin to see ourselves in only one light. This is our personal construct.

One of the aims of meditation is to transcend this socialization and overcome these limitations so that we might explore the full possibility of ourselves, go beyond our illusions about ourselves and the world (referred to as *maya* in the literature of Buddhist meditation), and attain the bliss state of Nirvana—enlightenment—in which we experience the full reality of who we actually are beyond who we have learned to be. In darkness this also seems possible.

As Lisa, a Darkness Visible participant, says:

Seeing in this way enabled me to access a deeper level of my consciousness and to experience the flow of energy outside me and within me at the same time. It allowed me to feel a connection outside of time and space.

This sounds strange to me because it isn't something I would believe if I hadn't experienced it for myself. I felt a deep sense of stillness, calm, and well-being, which grew as the darkness deepened. I felt my heart open up to a new dimension, a new way of seeing, feeling, and understanding myself and the world around me. I felt at peace. There was a sense of the sacred. . . . Emotions flowed freely through me without judgment or blockage—more tears and more joy, heartfelt and totally without judgment or fear; a calm acceptance that had a sense of beauty and serenity that I have not experienced before.

THE ISOLATED MIND

When you close your doors, and make darkness within, remember
never to say that you are alone, for you are not alone; nay, God is
within, and your genius is within. And what need have they of
light to see what you are doing?

EPICTETUS, *THE DISCOURSES OF EPICTETUS*
(ROBIN HARD TRANSLATION)

Although participants in Darkness Visible share a dark community made up of others who are part of their group and, in some way, also a part of their unique experience, the Mindfold they wear and their individual blindness lead to a sense of aloneness and a different way of understanding the world, which turns out to be protective and protecting, comforting and freeing.

This is alluded to by Cedric in his comment that within darkness there are "no visual incoming data to analyze, no body language, no gestures, looks, glances, [or] 'meaningful' stares." There is nothing to be (or pretend to be) except what we truly are, which can be freely expressed when others cannot see and judge us or demand that we be something else. Knowing also that the journey we are on is shared by others, there is a natural inclination toward appreciation and respect for the individual experience of those around us who are also alone in the dark.

In a way, this is the condition of every human being, sighted or otherwise, on our planet: we are all surrounded by others, but are simply trying to find our own way in the dark. We forget this in our normal lives, but in darkness it is quite apparent. This sense of shared humanity is echoed by another participant, who remarks that she "became more tolerant of people's differences" through the experience of darkness because she had to "rely on other senses to know them in a different way." Ironically, it is only when we are alone in the darkness that we finally see the unique beauty of everyone around us.

We know something of the other effects of isolation from studies conducted by NASA as well as research into flotation (isolation) tank experiences.

In *The Psychology of Isolation*, John Sturgeon writes of the psychological impact of time spent in the deep isolation of space. He also looks at research conducted at McGill University in Montreal, Canada (the "cornerstone to the foundation of isolation research"), which arose from the work of Donald Hebb.[7]

In his book *The Organization of Behavior*, Hebb reports that "uniform stimulation" (that is, lack of or reduced stimulation—as found in meditation or darkness work, for example) leads to "a degeneration in the ability to think and reason effectively."[8] By this Hebb means that the rational, "nonmythological" mind is disempowered or disengaged in some way when there is a reduction in stimulation from the outside world. This could, of course, lead to problems for astronauts in space; but for us in terms of this book, if Hebb is right, reduced stimulation should also lead to the emergence of a more emotive and nonrational experience in the psyche, just as meditative practices and immersions in darkness do.

Hebb began his studies at McGill, using twenty-two male college students as subjects, all of whom received twenty dollars a day to do precisely nothing. Great work if you can get it.

The subjects wore translucent goggles that allowed in diffuse light but prevented ordinary vision. By the second and third days the subjects began to report "difficulties in concentration" as the rational mind relaxed its hold on them, as well as "visual, kinesthetic [moving], and somasthetic [feeling] hallucinations."[9]

Such hallucinations are completely in keeping with the darkness experience as the mythological mind begins to flex its muscles and participants gain access to a wider and deeper awareness of their unconscious selves. Indeed, perhaps *hallucination* is not even the right word. Perhaps the experience of the limitless and unconditioned mind is naturally one of visionary experience and wider awareness, through images and symbols, of a much deeper and vaster connection to life.

Michael, a 2003 participant in the Darkness Visible retreat, speaks of this opening up of the visionary mind when he shares his own hallucinations:

> The general, dull black/amber visual jumble began to coalesce into discernible visions . . . initially cloudscapes. . . . Later I became aware of silhouetted fir trees that eventually formed into total mountain scenes . . . a rocky mountain ski area from high up on the trails, all lit by an amber light like a yellow moon that was always behind me and sometimes seemed to warm my back. Remarkably, it even cast a shadow where my feet would have been! Throughout, the warmth of the light source shone on my back and regularly cast the strange, disembodied shadow. There were other visions too.

Within the context of Sturgeon's NASA-oriented paper, Hebb's findings about the possible "degeneration" in rational processes is regarded as a potentially negative effect. After all, nobody would welcome astronauts in charge of billions of dollars of space-flight equipment to become "enlightened" in this way—not when they have a mission to complete and a spacecraft to land. As the research into this "degeneration" continued, however, more positive effects were also noted.

Sturgeon quotes a 1956 study by Vernon and Hoffman, for example ("Effects of Sensory Deprivation on Learning Rate in Human Beings," *Science* 123, no. 1074–75 [1956]), which involved subjects in a forty-eight-hour period of isolation and found that sensory deprivation actually enhanced the learning process by removing extraneous distractions. In our view, this enhanced learning is actually a *relearning;* we are being reprogrammed to accept our potential to learn. Further, the increased capacity to learn is not just due to the reduction in external stimuli; it is a natural effect of having more brainpower available as we get beyond the habitual 5 percent.

Sturgeon points out that "intellectual impairment . . . mental deficiencies . . . hallucinations are among the effects of confinement and isolation." Such "impairments" may, of course, present problems in space, and cosmonauts such as Yuri Gagarin have indeed reported decreased attention and concentration during space flights, when that rational 5 percent of brain function is most needed. But these effects are not a problem for deliberate voyagers into inner space. If we look at Sturgeon's comments from this perspective, we can see that what he is talking about is an increase in visionary potential and a decreased reliance on rational and habitual thought. In this sense, the reduction in external stimuli actually has a positive effect: an expansion of awareness and potential, giving us access to that unconscious 95 percent of ourselves.

Sturgeon notes other "problems" due to isolation, including "somatic complaints, sleep disturbances, [and] . . . changes in mood and morale." These are also consistent with the Darkness Visible experience: changes in the quality of sleeping (sleep is often deeper and more restful) and dreaming (dreams grow more vibrant and easier to remember), along with a greater connection to moods and emotions, are all experienced by our participants—although they do not regard these as problems, but rather as blessings. One participant, Alison, offers: "Visiting the darkness was like visiting a very close old friend. I felt immediately comfortable and relaxed. On an emotional level I was surprised as to how wonderfully safe and held I felt right from the outset."

The psychologists I. Altman and W. W. Haythorn reached a similar finding in their research into "performance effectiveness, stress reactions, and interpersonal exchange processes that occur in social isolation."[10] The results of their study show more honest self-disclosure, friendliness, and initiative among people in isolation than in a control group of others free to interact in a more familiar way. This is also our experience on our retreats.

The other realm in which we can learn about the psychological effects of isolation is that of flotation, sensory-deprivation, or isolation-tank experiments. The flotation tank, developed in 1953 by Dr. John Lilly at the National Institutes of Mental Health in Bethesda, Maryland, comprises a sealed container of salinated water at body temperature. The user floats in womblike darkness, buoyed by the water, which creates a feeling of dissolving into the surroundings.

Using the tank, Lilly explored how isolated states affect consciousness. What he discovered was a powerful means of transcending self-limiting beliefs that is "startlingly similar to the shamanic or visionary state—the darkness, the silence [another component of Darkness Visible work, during which participants spend at least one day in silence], the sense of relaxation and focus on the self, as well as the visions and sensations that arise from these two specific uses of the mind and body."[11]

Lilly's findings show that the activity of the brain is slowed during isolation in the tank, allowing the user to bypass the rational and analytical mind. The individual experiences a shift into deeper levels of the unconscious, feeling, and creative mind, where more intuitive and dreaming aspects of the self emerge.

Scientifically speaking, when external stimuli are less available to the hypothalamic, pituitary, and brain-stem regions of the central nervous system, as is the case in darkness or within a flotation tank, the reticular formation and its activating system—nerve fibers within the brain stem that regulate motor functions and normal awareness—relax. Further, the body's production of ACTH (adrenocorticotropic hormone)—a substance that readies us for action—is inhibited, preventing stimulation of the autonomic nervous system. This in turn inhibits the release of the neurotransmitters epinephrine and norepinephrine, which are associated with tension and anxiety. All of this results in deeper levels of relaxation. Heart rate decreases, the brain's electrical activity slows, and alpha and theta brain waves, associated with deep states of meditation, begin to appear. At the same time, encephalons, which have a molecular structure similar to morphine and are more commonly known as endorphins (endogenous morphines), are produced in the brain and released into the body. These are the body's natural painkillers and produce a sense of well-being and euphoria.

In general, then, people feel physically better, healed, less anxious, and more in touch with the natural and full state of their bodies during periods of isolation and subsequent introspection—which we can verify from our own darkness experience and from receiving feedback on the experiences of retreat participants:

> Throughout the whole time I was in darkness, I had no physical pain. For many months I have suffered with a pain in my lower back on the right side and also a pain in my left knee, but I felt no physical pain at all throughout the whole retreat. My body felt healthy and wonderful—no aches . . . not even a twitch. I totally relaxed. I felt calmer and more at peace [and] the darkness stilled and quieted my mind.
>
> When I took the blindfold off [however], within a couple of hours the pain in my side and my knee returned.

This healing also extends to more emotional or psycho-spiritual wounds:

> I found peace from my own inner wars. It was the first time I had been gentle and kind to myself in many years. I was more in touch with my body [and] could feel sometimes even past my body—feeling and knowing with my whole being where I was and what I was doing. Even eating became a sacred act of feeding the body with love.

(Readers will find more on the healing aspects of darkness in chapters 6 and 7.)

What else happens to people during times of sensory deprivation? They have visions, and these may be meaningful, significant, and healing in themselves. Like the shamans in trance within their dark initiatory caves, new realms of possibility open up for people as they merge with a place within themselves that is much deeper than everyday consciousness. Michael Hutchinson, in *The Book of Floating*, which is about the isolation-tank experience, describes this place as one of "sudden insight, creative inspiration . . . a mysterious, elusive state" that can provide us with "integrative experiences leading to psychological well-being."[12]

This imaginative state induces visions that are not just random, but carry useful information for us and, what's more, will naturally produce (or can be guided to yield) helpful physical effects. Dr. Edmund Jacobson, for example, demonstrated a link between mental imagery and bodily effects that shows that we can change ourselves physically using the power of the mind alone. Jacobson asked people to visualize themselves running and then measured muscle movement in response to their images. He found that their movements were essentially the same as if they were actually running and that the body received the health-giving benefits of this mental jog.[13]

Allied to this is the work of Alan Richardson, who, in his research into the power of visionary states, asked one group of schoolchildren to practice basketball throws each day and a second group to simply visualize making perfect shots but not actually practice. Twenty days later the first group showed a 24 percent performance improvement, while the second group, the members of which hadn't even picked up a ball, showed a 23 percent improvement—not much below those who had been shooting hoops for twenty days.[14]

In other words, when the mind perceives an event, image, or action as real, it generates physical responses as if it were real. The result is that it becomes real. By extrapolation, if we imagine ourselves as infinitely powerful, supernaturally healthy, emotionally healed, or at one with the universe (typical participant experiences as a result of their darkness work), then we become these.

Remarkable in this respect is the work of John Basmajian who, through biofeedback measurements, has demonstrated that human beings in visionary states of active imagination can even control their autonomic nervous systems (once thought to be beyond human control), right down to the firing of one specific neuron in their bodies, a feat that has been described by some scientists as "more difficult than finding a single grain of sand in a desert."[15]

Following from this is the work of Dr. Carl Simonton of the Cancer Counseling and Research Center in Fort Worth, Texas, who uses images to help his patients control and heal their cancers. He finds that by asking patients to visualize themselves winning the war against cancer, they are able to live twice as long as those who are not using vision in their healing. What's more, many of them recover fully through otherwise inexplicable remissions.[16]

Surely then, it is worth asking what positive effects darkness therapy could add to the healing process, given that darkness itself tends to stimulate the brain's image-producing function and capacities for health-giving relaxation, and that, as we also know from our workshops, these images can be guided in particular and specific directions to produce useful outcomes for participants.

The use (or perhaps, the natural effects) of images produced in this way also has something in common with the notion of *flow*, a term developed by Mihaly Csikszentmihalyi of the University of Chicago and defined by the process of completing naturally, miraculously, and very easily an action that we usually find to be difficult or impossible. Flow is the experience of the athlete "in the zone" and the sensation we all have perhaps had at one time or another that we don't really need to work at a task in order to force our achievements or healings or self-realizations; instead, they simply happen and we simply allow them to do so. Perhaps this is the natural potential of all of us all of the time if we can master, or simply give free rein to, more of that 95 percent of our active unconscious that we normally don't touch.

In flow, this state of relaxed allowing of our own capabilities, we have "no active awareness of control but [are] simply not worried about the possibility of lack of control. Later, in thinking back on the experience, [an individual in flow] will usually conclude that his skills were adequate for meeting environmental demands, and this reflection might become an important component of a private self-concept."[17]

In other words, the experience itself of being in a state of enhanced awareness and of having access to uncharted but entirely natural human skills informs us of our potential and, through this, raises that potential so that we are even more available to success. As Joseph Campbell reminds us, "The adventure is the reward in itself."

All of this—the appearance of healing visions, the enhanced connection with and understanding of the body, the sensation of flow—is manifestly present in darkness and brings long-term benefits in its wake.

Alison offers this:

> I fell into the joy of darkness instantly. My sensing involved my whole being on a very physical level [and] I became aware of myself as motion and stillness, a flow of energy.
>
> What was particularly fascinating was that, far from being a spiritual or esoteric experience, it was completely present in my physical being in a way I have never experienced before.
>
> The experience of this work has been so deeply profound that it has challenged my fundamental understanding of my being . . . I feel that there has been a shift on a cellular/DNA level. Just about everything in life has changed on every level. . . . My authentic self awoke fully and she wants to taste the world she now inhabits!

Alison's account is lyrical and beautiful, but the simple words of another participant are equally moving and reveal just as well the sense of enhanced connection—the feeling of *more*—and the expansion of being that comes from darkness so that we can effortlessly feel ourselves to be part of the infinite, beyond our self-limited human shell: "I feel a greater affinity with nature now. I actually feel a part of it. This is not a logical brain process but an inexplicable feeling."

There is one final area of psychology and neuroscience that may be pertinent to darkness work: current research into a condition called Charles Bonnet Syndrome (CBS). *Psychology Today* was one of the first journals to carry a story on this condition:

> Harry's nearly 73 and his eyesight isn't what it was. But psychologically he's completely normal. So why is he seeing people, buildings, and shrubs that aren't really there?
>
> The answer has nothing to do with schizophrenia, LSD, or any of the usual causes of hallucinations. Harry's plight is due to a little known—and surprisingly common—condition called Charles Bonnet Syndrome. People with CBS are mentally sound in every way—except they occasionally see things that don't exist.[18]

In a study of these unexplained visions—all of them among elderly patients, who, incidentally, were people for whom darkness was natural, given their failing eyesight—scientists found that one in seven hallucinated. Mainly their visions were of mundane things, such as the faces of strangers, although some saw nonhuman, spiritlike, or archetypal entities, such as humanoid creatures dressed in tree branches.

Where do these images come from in people who are otherwise psychologically normal? According to the article in *Psychology Today*, the experience of darkness is indeed key, given that the eyesight of most CBS patients functions at less than one third of normal capacity. "People in sensory deprivation tanks start hallucinating after a couple of hours in isolation," Robert Teunisse, M.D., notes in the article, and something similar might also occur in CBS sufferers.

Once again, we learn that darkness brings visions. It is possible, then, that if CBS patients were taught to deliberately access and explore these, they might discover, as medical doctors such as Carl Simonton have learned, that such visions can be welcomed as healing and empowering, rather than considered as hallucinations to be feared or cured. After all, we have the whole universe within us—it is only our habits of thought that prevent us from knowing this. What miracles, then, might we be capable of if we let in darkness?

TRY THIS
The Voices Within

Whenever we sit down quietly and close our eyes to meditate, we are likely to encounter distractions from a number of voices, often deeply layered, within our heads. Some of these are the critic, the parent, and the observer or "scientist." They are the old programs we carry: instructions or descriptions from the people in our past who have had some influence over us and that, even now, still affect us by causing us to hear ourselves (and then to behave) in the ways they dictate.

Whose voices do you hear when you close your eyes? Know that these are not your voice and that what they tell you is not who or what you truly are and certainly not all you can be. Nonetheless, listen anyway to what they have to say. Give each voice a name and personality so you can recognize them when they appear.

All of these voices have useful information for us, mostly about how we are limiting ourselves by buying into old patterns from people who once had power over us.

Talk with these different voices, if you wish, in the same way you talked with God in the exercise "Forgiving God" on page 17. In this way, you can reach an agreement with these nags from the past so that they will not keep pushing themselves forward and you will not have to carry them into the future. (Also see the exercise "Your Conception/Life Story" on page 111 for further insight into where some of your internal voices might come from.)

◐ Active Imagining: Using Darkness for Positive Change

Research suggests that the active imagination can be employed to make practical and positive changes in all areas of our lives—from basketball throws to cancer treatments. Perhaps there is something in your life that you'd like to change or a skill you'd like to develop.

Close your eyes and see yourself succeeding in whatever task you have in mind. Rehearse it thoroughly and be truly present as you do. Let your body move as it would in the situation you imagine. Allow your senses to experience the reality of the scene: Make any sounds you would naturally make; if there is a crowd, hear its roar. Familiarize yourself with the territory as precisely as you can so that when you actually face this challenge, it is easy to be present.

If tackling your imagined task can be measured in reality—such as, say, an improvement in performance in a particular sport or on a musical instrument—go ahead and test yourself, if you feel comfortable doing so. Measure your performance before your visualization, then practice in your imaging for a week or so, and measure your performance again. Do you note any improvement?

◐ The Flow of Things

I said to my soul, be still, and wait without hope
For hope would be hope for the wrong thing;
Wait without love, for love would be love of the wrong thing...
Wait without thought, for you are not ready for thought;
So the darkness shall be the light, and the stillness the dancing.

T. S. ELIOT

It is human inclination to form attachments, to hold on to what we had or have or the desire for what we want in the future. Once we get caught up in our wants for the future, it is also natural to overlook what we already have, though we may cling to it so that it cannot be taken from us. We may also rely on the past or future for inspiration on what to do next. All in all, we rarely live in the Now, as we hope for things, building dreams around what may or may not be, search for unconditional love, and then attach our own terms and conditions to what we find. Finally, we think too much!

This is not the experience of flow, that exhilarating feeling of being in the moment, attached to nothing, understanding ourselves as part of everything. In flow we don't hope because we are already living our potential; we don't love because we *are* love; we don't think because we are beyond thinking. We're literally out of our minds and in our bliss. All of this is possible, time and again, if we let ourselves go and let go of the things that hold us to the earth.

Close your eyes and let an image form of all the things that hold you in place right now—attachments to people, possessions, security, status—as if they were ropes fixed to your body and weighted down by rocks. Then, one by one begin to lift the rocks and move them away.

Don't be afraid as you do this: it doesn't mean you can't have these things again, if you choose; it simply means you'll be able to take them back on your own terms.

Feel how much lighter your body becomes without all of this weight pinning you to the ground!

5

Entering the Dark World
Initiation into Darkness

> *The instruments of darkness tell us truths.*
>
> MACBETH I:3

THE EFFECTS OF darkness can be liberating and healing, as we have seen, but what is it that first calls people to this experience?

Why would anyone rationally choose to go without sight for five days and nights or longer, to put themselves willingly through the challenges, confusions, and paradoxes that arise during this amount of time in darkness? What is it that drives people into the dark?

The answer: their need for initiation. *Initiation* is a word we often hear participants use spontaneously when they express interest in stepping into darkness. It is not a concept we suggest to them, but rather one they relay to us. Kevin speaks for many participants in this respect when he remarks: "I saw Darkness Visible as an initiation, of which I was much in need."

All initiations into the mysteries of life have traditionally taken place in dark spaces. The Orphic rituals of ancient Greece were enacted in caves. The Egyptians held their rites and rituals of rebirth in dark tombs within pyramids. In Haiti, it is into the dark inner sanctum of the Vodou temple that the priest-to-be is led while blindfolded.

One rare account of initiation into the classical mysteries—in this case, the Egyptian mysteries of Isis—is given in *The Golden Ass,* a Latin "novel" written by Apuleius in the second century C.E.

> I approached the very gates of death and set one foot on Proserpine's threshold yet was permitted to return, borne through all the elements. At midnight I saw the sun shining as if it were noon: I entered the presence of the Gods of the underworld and the Gods of the upper world, stood near and worshipped them.[1]

In the classical mysteries, this light within the earth, found through journeying in darkness, was known as the Sun at Midnight, suggesting life-changing sight in darkness or a means of seeing the true nature of the self.

In modern society we all live in the dark, so to speak, most of the time—the world has become so big and cumbersome, so separate and beyond us. At the same time, its workings seem so subtle and based on secrets, intrigue, diplomatic nuances, power politics, economics, rules, policies, plans, and procedures that we do not know it anymore. Yet we are never initiated into its mysteries; we never learn to understand the energies and forces that lie beneath and drive our world or how we, as human beings, can respond to these. It is answers that we seek, along with some insights into how we should live.

Our need to know is no different today than it ever was. Anthropologists betray their own fascination with the processes of initiation when they record (as most books of anthropology inevitably do) the exotic practices of peoples across the globe who have carried out tribal initiations for thousands of years. Archaeologists have discovered ritual objects used in such ceremonies dating back 400,000 years. In the first part of the last century, a series of initiatory grottoes used by our distant ancestors in Neanderthal times was discovered in the high mountains of Switzerland, also testifying to the force of the mythic imagination and the power of initiation in the ordering of their lives.

The world has changed dramatically since then, but our human physiology, our concerns and passions—the landscapes of our souls and our psyches—are essentially the same. As we were no doubt driven then, we are driven now by the questions: Who am I? Why am I here? Where am I going? Who am I to become? We still need to know these things, to feel welcome in the world and to find our place within it.

In simpler times, initiation was the central practice of all societies: Boys or girls of appropriate age were taken from the group and immersed in a very different or "other" way of being so that they might discover maturity, responsibility, and power. These individuals were then returned—as adults—to the tribe, which regarded them now as people who had touched their potential and the genius within themselves and could contribute to their community in a more mature and effective way. They had faced their challenges and could truly say: "I am a man!" or "I am a woman!"—"I Am!"—and know what these words meant.

Such boys and girls had faced mysteries through trials, challenges, and inner seeking and had discovered personal realizations about the nature of the world and what it means to be human. They returned from their initiation experience with discoveries to teach about the world "out there," beyond conventional life.

So hungry are we, in our modern world, for initiatory rites such as these, presented to us in a useful way by tribal elders who know how to manage such powerful processes, that we will make them up—sometimes with frightening consequences. Robert Moore and Douglas Gillette, in *King, Warrior, Magician, Lover,* for example, speak of our culture's pseudorituals, such as violent inductions into street gangs, which may, in some cases, require that would-be gang members commit murder in order to prove themselves. The result of such desperate and unguided modern processes is that initiates become "skewed, stunted, and false . . . abusive of others, and often of self. . . ." This, the authors contend, is at the root of all social problems today.[2]

Many of us are lost or confused in our modern world. We have no elders to guide us, to show us the way into manhood or womanhood, to help us uncover the secrets we keep and discover the power within us, to introduce us to the sacred, or to give us the means to vision and to a more authentic life. At best, we have the "nanny" state to care for us, to give us *rights* (instead of *rites*), which we must exercise with a presumed, rather than a felt, maturity. We see the consequences of this presumption, somewhere down the line, in the form of men and women who do not actually know themselves, who are in many ways still children looking for guidance and answers from wisdom keepers who do not exist. A real initiation, by contrast, is a graduation into wholeness and adulthood. Initiates emerge with access to a wisdom and strength they did not know before.

Interestingly, even when our participants do not directly use the word *initiation,* their need for such a ritual is implied. Mike, for example, asked why he wants to be part of our workshops, explains his motivation simply as a hope "to learn." Though he does not say exactly what it is he hopes to learn, his need is deep and powerful enough to bring him to an experience that he knows will involve a dramatic encounter with his inner world and the personal myths of his life. It is *himself* that Mike needs to learn about—it could be nothing else, for nothing else is on offer at a Darkness Visible retreat. Who am I? Why am I here? What is the purpose of this life?: these age-old questions are at the heart of every initiation, and Mike hopes to learn the answers to them.

The same drive is there for others as well: "I was very attracted to work in darkness, for it was something I feared from [childhood]. I wanted the opportunity to meet with darkness to help [overcome] that fear and [find] love for myself."

What these words speak of is our need to reach beyond what we know—and know to have failed for us. We long to face a new challenge and break through to a new way of seeing, overcoming fears, or finding a vision, a way based on personal experience instead of hand-me-down information from a society that offers only pseudorituals.

Our participants' comments are the words of hero-children about to go into battle on the field of the soul and emerge, we hope, as men or women of power who have proved themselves to themselves. What they are really seeking is an opportunity—the battleground itself—to begin the fight to discover who they are.

All initiations—including that of Darkness Visible retreats—have three stages:

1. First, there is a time of unknowing, when initiates leave the past behind, letting go of illusions that do not serve them. It is a time of separating from the known or the "normal" and of opening to possibilities. For Darkness Visible participants this may begin weeks in advance of the retreat itself, when they first decide to embark on this experience, but certainly begins at the moment they put on their Mindfold and enter the dark world outside of their usual reality, where time and space and the rational mind will cease to exist for them in the days ahead.

2. Next comes the warrior's challenge, a time for initiates to face fears and tackle the obstacles to growth, to prove themselves through action and commitment. On Darkness Visible retreats this stage is represented by the exercises we assign our participants and the opportunities they have to experience the world anew. Some of these exercises are deeply introspective and engender a questioning not only of social reality but of the myths behind the lives they have been living.

3. Finally, initiates reach the homecoming, a celebration of themselves for having explored the deeper mysteries of the self and tasted the magic of a more awakened life and emerged newborn from this experience.

For our participants, this threefold process formally begins as they sit in circle and individually step forward to ritually enter the darkness by putting on their Mindfolds. What do these initiates make of their steps into the dark? For most, it is actually a relief, as if this moment were one they have been waiting for all their lives and finally—*finally!*—their time of initiation has arrived. Here are some comments participants have shared:

> My personal experience was one of visceral readiness to leap into that to which I had so strongly been called.

[I felt] feelings of excitement and adventure.

I felt ready when it came time to put on the blindfold. I *wanted* to enter darkness and was ready to step into an adventure, a journey and a new dimension. . . . Stepping into the darkness was like taking a leap of faith into the unknown. . . . I relaxed into trust, a sense of hope, and safety.

Almost as soon as participants enter darkness, their relationship to the world begins to change. Senses expand: taste, smell, touch, and hearing all become more vibrant. Ordinary, familiar details in nature, such as the warmth of the sun, the touch of a leaf, the wind in the trees, or the feeling of earth, seem suddenly different and somehow more sacred, as if they were in some way closer and could be appreciated more fully.

Most significant, however, is how participants in darkness relate to one another contrasted with how they related before they were blindfolded. As all of them enter darkness, a community of shared interest, intention, or involvement in the sacred is instantly formed. They have all gone beyond the mundane world to become the elect, pilgrims in another land experiencing the numinous. Their two overriding responses to this are awe at their new world and a deeper level of trust for one another in the knowledge that their experience and awe are shared.

The relationship between all in the dark community changed dramatically. Everyone helped each other and there was an instant bond and friendship between all. I felt honored, for I was on occasions able to help the others and I also knew that they would help me if I was "lost." I had 100 percent faith and trust—the 100 percent trust that I do not give to others normally.

My sense of touch was much sharper and so many things were really wonderful to just feel. I smelled things much finer and the food tasted exquisite. It was like I could taste every ingredient more fully than ever before. My sense of hearing also became sharper. I remember listening to some of the music that was played in the evenings and having amazing, powerful, and raw emotions surface: pain, grief, sadness, joy, and love. All these feelings came at different times. My senses were heightened to the wind and the temperature and, just by feeling, I knew if I was in sunlight.

Nature held a new fascination that I cannot put across in words. Thinking back, it was, for me, a first real connection with nature on a spiritual level.

Other participants remark:

I felt an immediate trust and sense of community as we were all drawn to be doing this extraordinary work at this time in this place. I felt a particular resonance with my buddy [every participant is assigned a buddy, or work partner], which continues to this day.

Emotion wrote its own script as, being in darkness, there were no restraints. It felt as though the world was more alive than it normally feels. [My sense of] smell became more acute. [My sense of] touch expanded its awareness considerably . . . cold felt prickly, warm felt smooth. [My] hearing became more acute as I put a great deal of awareness into sound.

There was a lovely group bonding, unhindered and uncomplicated by the visual cues that normally carry our societal and sexual prejudices [and] I was aware of the disintegration of our social/physical boundaries. . . . Emotionally, I felt free and open. The most fascinating and wonderful sensation was of the earth beneath my feet and all around me.

Emotions flowed freely through me without judgment or blockage. Ordinary and natural things like sunlight and breeze . . . were more intense and I was aware of the fiber of things and the flow of energy, which connected everything. I became quieter and felt more at peace with myself. It also felt good to link up with others by touch rather than words and [this] allowed a sense of connection based on acceptance and truth rather than judgment. I became more tolerant of people's differences and relied on other senses to know them in a different way.

DEEPENING INTO DARKNESS

When your eyes are closed to distracting phenomena, you're in your intuition, and you may come in touch with the morphology, the basic form of things.

JOSEPH CAMPBELL, *REFLECTIONS ON THE ART OF LIVING*

The ritual application of the Mindfold on Darkness Visible retreats represents the descent into the mystery of initiation, while the workshop exercises that follow represent aspects of the "warrior's challenge": trials, in a sense, that the participant must overcome during his or her time in darkness.

In the following chapters we discuss some of these exercises to show how they relate to a deepening of the darkness experience and what participants learn from them about the reality of their existence beyond social convention and accepted notions of what it true.

There is another important aspect of initiation, though, that we should first discuss: every initiation is also a death. In Haiti, as the blindfold is placed over initiates' eyes and they are led into the darkened temple to experience the mysteries, the women of the village begin to cry: "My children, my children, they are killing my children." The ritual is designed so that initiates have a sense of their death to the old ways of the world and rebirth into a new order of things.

It is the same in other tribal cultures. In Australia, the elders may one day seize a boy who is ready to be initiated into manhood. Each elder appears in his spirit form, naked except for white feathers stuck to his skin using the "glue" of his own blood, symbolizing that this is an ancient and arcane ritual that transcends even matters of life and death and involves both the visible and invisible worlds.

The elders swing bull-roarers, the voice of the spirits, as they snatch the boy away from his mother and take him to the sacred grounds. There, he goes through ritual ordeals, including subincision, circumcision, and drinking the blood of the elders, while he is instructed in the lore and legends of his tribe and the spiritual universe of which it and he are a part.

At the end of this process, the young boy is deemed to have died, but he returns to his village as a man who understands the mystery behind the material. Waiting for him is a woman who has been selected to become his bride. Adult life begins for him then and there.

Sometimes this notion of dying to the old, manifested by the integration of death with these rites, does not operate simply on a symbolic level. In New Guinea, following a five-day ritual, initiate boys are taken into a loosely built log shed in which a woman waits so they may have their first sexual experience of manhood. The woman is dressed as a deity, representing the sacred that is in all flesh. The boys have sex with her one at a time and so become gods.

When the last of them is in union with this woman, the logs supporting the fragile shed are deliberately removed so the hut collapses and the man and woman are crushed—the new man-god and woman-goddess in perfect congress forever. Their bodies are then removed from the wreckage and they are roasted and eaten. For the tribe, this is a form of Mass, the ingestion of the divine. Future Darkness Visible participants will be comforted to know that our insurance does not cover this aspect of ritual, and our approach to the death-rebirth process therefore remains at a more symbolic ceremonial level than that of the New Guinea tribesmen.

In particular, the death-rebirth aspect of the Darkness Visible initiation is represented in a series of three separate but interlinking exercises—"The Conception Journey," "Who Are You?," and "Earth's Embrace"—presented in the following chapter.

The notion behind these exercises is that we all assemble our lives from information that has been presented to us by circumstances or by influential people such as our parents and teachers, and that we have chosen, at some level, to buy into—that is, from all the millions of bits of data, words, images, and behaviors that we might absorb, hear, or observe in relation to ourselves, we have selected some that we regard as more significant than others and have built a life around them. This is what DelMonte refers to as a "construct" of ourselves (see page 65). We experience who we are on a mythological level, living out life stories that are literally that: *stories* we have made up about ourselves and now accept as fact because they have become a part of our habitual response to the world.

The three exercises are a means for participants to make these stories obvious and conscious to themselves, to reassess the data of their lives from which these stories arose, and to seize an opportunity to change them, if they wish, now that they are aware of these personal myths.

Before moving on to the trilogy of exercises in chapter 6, though, I present some exercises here based on the fundamental elements of initiation.

TRY THIS
⬤ The Wise Elder

Initiations within tribal or indigenous cultures have always been carried out by elders—men or women who have themselves been initiated into the mysteries of life and can thus guide their students with competence. These days, elders are few and far between.

Yet somewhere within us we have access to ancestral memories that connect us to more ancient times when such initiations were a way of life for all human beings. We all have an innate sense, then, of what such elders might look like or what they might offer us.

Close your eyes and see yourself back in the cave you visited in the exercise "The Cave of Souls" (page 35). You stand before a tunnel you have not yet explored. Step into it now. There, you will find a wise and loving being, someone who has always known you—the deep you, the you that you hide even from yourself; a being who loves you dearly and has your best interests at heart. Perhaps it is an ancestor, an initiated man or woman from your family clan; perhaps it is a tribal elder, a shaman, a sage.

Do you have any questions you would like to ask of this wise being? Are there any answers you need about any aspect of your life? Ask away—and know you can always return if you need further advice.

At the end of this consultation, you may find that the elder has a gift for you that will help you live in a better way. What is this gift? How does it relate to you? How will you use it purposefully in your life?

Retrace your steps back to the entrance to the tunnel and open your eyes.

◐ Dying to Live

Initiation has sometimes been seen as a form of useful death, a means of dying to the old or letting go of what was, so that something new can emerge.

Many traditional peoples see the wisdom of viewing death in this way—not as something to be feared, but as a transformational agent. One practice incorporating this view involves imagining that you are about to die this instant and that you will be measured and remembered by your immediate response to the last question asked of you, the final demand you make, the last action you take, and so on. What would you answer, ask for, or do if you knew your time here was coming to an end?

Now close your eyes and remember—without judgment, guilt, or shame—a decision you made in the past. What might you have done instead if you had known it was your last?

Now step back into the present. What choices or decisions do you have to make now? Knowing that every one of them could be the last you will make on Earth, what will you decide?

◐ Rebirth

As well as a symbolic death, every initiation is a new beginning, a chance to dream a new world.

Imagine you have died right now and can start again. What does this new and perfect world and life look like? Close your eyes and explore it.

What's stopping you from making this your world and life right now?

6

The Stories of Our Lives
Exploring the Dark Self

Through every rift of discovery some seeming anomaly drops
out of the darkness, and falls, as a golden link, into the
great chain of order.

EDWIN HUBBEL CHAPIN

ACCEPTED MEDICAL OPINION tells us we have few memories of our lives before the age of five because the memory centers of our brains do not develop much before then. Recent research, however, suggests this view of our development is very far from the truth. In fact, the stories by which we will come to define ourselves arise not from interactions with the social world, but from the womb itself.

The myths we live by may begin before we are even conceived, and the development of memory centers in our brains is quite irrelevant to this process. Scientist Karl Pribram suggests, for example, that the brain itself is not very significant with regard to memory; that our entire body, not our brain alone, contains memories, with every part storing information. In fact, rats who have been taught by Pribram to run a maze, then have the memory centers of their brains removed, still remember their way around the maze.

We have also recently learned that the gut has its own "brain" (the enteric nervous system, or ENS), with as many nerve fibers as the brain in our head and one hundred million neurons—more than are in the spinal cord.

The ENS is a single connected entity located in the lining of the esophagus, stomach, small intestine, and colon, with its own network of neurons, neurotransmitters, and proteins. Nearly every substance in the brain is also present in the gut, including serotonin, dopamine, norepinephrine, enkephalins, benzodiazepines, and brain proteins called neuropeptides. This "brain" is therefore able to learn, remember, sense from its environment, feel, and respond—all quite independently from the brain in our head.

Furthermore, the brain in the gut and the brain in the head act in exactly the same way when they are deprived of input from the outside world. During deep meditation or sleep, for example, the brain in the head produces ninety-minute cycles of slow-wave activity punctuated with dream sleep characterized by rapid eye movement (REM). At the same time, the brain in the gut produces ninety-minute cycles of slow-wave muscle contractions punctuated by bursts of rapid muscle movement.

Researchers have also found that the brain in the gut plays a significant role in our experience of emotions such as joy and sadness, which are revealed in a metaphorical, image-based way. The mood comes first, and then, if we tune in to what our gut instinct is telling us, a picture begins to emerge of the meaning behind the feeling.

We also know that these two brains develop independently as the fetus grows in the womb and only later become connected via the vagus nerve—important information for us in terms of the discussion of the origin of our learning. Thus, whenever we have a "gut reaction" to events, we may, in fact, be tuning in to our earliest emotional memories of joy or pain, fight or flight, from a time before we had a brain in our head or words to describe our feelings.*

---

*More information on the brain in the gut can be found in an article by Sandra Blakeslee entitled "Complex and Hidden Brain in the Gut Makes Cramps, Butterflies, and Valium," *New York Times*, 23 January, 1996.

On top of this, a range of psychological research has demonstrated a tangible connection between mothers (and fathers) and their children, due entirely to the womb experience. For example, mothers who have emotional problems during pregnancy may pass these on to their children in utero, who themselves manifest the same emotional problems immediately after birth. A mother whose pregnancy is deliberate, then, because she wants a child and has love to give, is offering her baby a different quality of experience in the womb than a mother who becomes pregnant by accident and worries about the consequences.

In the first case we can imagine an energy of love surrounding the growing fetus, with the mother taking more care during pregnancy to eat the right foods, avoid alcohol, and get enough exercise, because the mother's attention is focused on the health and happiness of her child. In the second case, stress and anxiety are likely to cause unhelpful changes in body chemistry (such as the release of excess levels of adrenaline) and these will reach the child through the blood that it shares with its mother. Biological science, as well as common sense, tells us that each child will form differently in the womb as a consequence of each experience—and this is just the beginning of the story of each child's life.

Even before our time in the womb, the expectation and dreaming that went into the creation of us as children produced a reaction in the minds and bodies of our parents, which became an important part of our making. Some people dream of a baby to the point of having the name of their unborn child in their minds for years before they actually conceive. Our names are highly significant because they represent an archetypal projection onto us by our parents of certain qualities that they viewed as desirable for us to have. Likewise, our names, to some extent, determine our life experiences, given that certain images pop into people's minds when they hear specific names.

All of this goes into the melting pot of who we are as we develop and, according to scientists such as Pribram, will be stored somewhere within us even if the memory center of our brain has not yet formed. To take this a step further, it may well be true that few of us really know who we are at a deeper level because we have been living someone else's dream (or story) of ourselves. This is only compounded at birth, when we begin to experience more formal socialization into the ways of the world and more labels and definitions are applied to us by others.

What follows are two techniques—"The Conception Journey" and "Who Are You"—that are used in conjunction in our Darkness Visible retreats to help participants understand themselves better through understanding their own conception, time in utero, and birth—including, as a major component, their parents' feelings throughout the process.

> *Our wisdom is not thin and clear like water, but thick*
> *and dark like blood.*
>
> THE BEE MISTRESS IN SIMON BUXTON'S
> *THE SHAMANIC WAY OF THE BEE*

THE CONCEPTION JOURNEY

The Conception Journey is a technique we use in Darkness Visible retreats to allow our participants to explore the personal mythologies they are living. It is a long meditation/visualization, which, like all exercises on this retreat, is performed in darkness.

Participants are first taken through a relaxation so they can focus on the work to be done. The text of the journey is then read aloud to them, and they follow the action through visualization and by tuning in to the truth of their feelings.

We have included a shortened form of it here so you can undertake it for yourself.* Because the exercise is still quite lengthy, however, we have suggested a number of break points throughout, which you can use as opportunities to write down your thoughts and recollections. If you wish, you can also take some time—an hour or a day—between each part.

---

*An expanded version of this exercise appears in the book *The Spiritual Practices of the Ninja* by Ross Heaven. Credit for helping to devise this meditation must also go to Howard G. Charing of the Eagle's Wing Centre for Contemporary Shamanism (shamanism.co.uk).

To begin with, lie down comfortably and empty your mind of conscious thought. Breathe in to your whole body, where (according to scientists like Pribram) your memories—including those that are preconscious—are actually stored, and then direct the breath to your stomach area, where the brain in your gut, the "feeling brain," is located. Relax into your breathing and tune in to your body.

Now allow yourself to merge with the consciousness of your father at a time before you were even conceived. Imagine him as a young man. Then let yourself become him as the person he was then, before you became his son or daughter. Why might you have chosen him as a father? What are his hopes, fears, ambitions, and regrets—for himself and for you? Are these hopes, fears, ambitions, and regrets in any way familiar to you in your life now? Close your eyes and explore the answers to these questions. Note any images that come to mind and any feelings and sensations that arise.

Now see your mother at a time before you were conceived and, in the same way, merge with her consciousness. Again, close your eyes and imagine the answers to the following questions and any subsequent feelings that arise: Why might you have chosen her as a mother? What are her hopes, fears, ambitions, regrets? Are these in any way familiar to you?

Now imagine your parents after they have met each other and made a decision (conscious or otherwise) to have a child together. We join them at the moment of their lovemaking that leads to your conception.

Allow yourself to merge with the consciousness of your father's sperm as it is released from his body and begins the journey that is the story of your life. What feelings, hopes, and fears are contained within this sperm? Now allow yourself to merge with the consciousness of your mother's egg. What feelings, hopes, and fears do you notice here? Are any of these feelings familiar to you now?

The egg and sperm come together in the moment of conception and a new consciousness is created: you. What characterizes this meeting between sperm and egg? How do they both feel at this meeting of their individual hopes, fears, and dreams? Are these feelings in any way familiar to you now (for example, in partnerships or relationships in your life)?

What are your feelings at this moment of your conception? What do you already know about yourself, this body of yours, this world around you, and the life you are destined to lead?

Record your observations up to this point in the exercise.

Now we have moved on in time once more and your mother and father are aware that they are pregnant with you. What are their feelings about this discovery? Has anything changed in their relationship or their feelings toward each other now that they are aware of this pregnancy? What are their feelings toward you? Have these changed now that you are a real event, not just a dream or idea? Imagine you are in your mother's womb. As a conscious life now, with feelings of your own, what is your reaction to the emotions you sense around you? Are these feelings familiar to you now, in your adult life, in the patterns within your relationships?

Again we move ahead in time to imagine your mother's first contraction in the process of your birth. What are her thoughts, feelings, and actions at this time? What are your father's thoughts, feelings, and actions? What are your feelings and actions as you sense this first contraction from within your mother's womb? Do any of these feelings and reactions (for example, to any occurrence in your life that may be sudden or unexpected) seem in any way familiar in your life now?

Record your observations on this part of the exercise.

Next, imagine you are now born and look around you, conscious, aware of your surroundings. How does the world look to you? How do you feel?

You see your mother and father for the first time. What are their feelings toward you? What are your feelings toward them? What are the first words you hear? What are your first thoughts about this world into which you have been born?

Now imagine your umbilical cord has been cut. What is your first feeling in response to this? Your first action? Do these seem in any way familiar to you now—perhaps, for example, when you are facing a situation in which you gain freedom or are separated from someone?

Record your observations on this part of the exercise.

Next, imagine you are an infant. What are your first needs? Are these met or unmet? What conscious or unconscious judgments do you make about yourself/your parents/the world around you as a consequence of having your needs met or unmet?

You are given food for the first time. Is this because you request it or because your mother automatically feeds you? What are your reactions to this first feeding?

We all make unconscious contracts with our parents, some of which may be contradictory or paradoxical in nature: "If I am sweet and do not cry, you will love and take care of me" or "If I cry loudly to get my needs met, you will love and take care of me." What was your contract with mother—and her contract with you? What was your contract with your father and his with you? Were these contracts honored by you? By your mother and father? Are these relationship contracts and their outcomes in any way familiar to you in your relationships now?

Record your observations on this part of the exercise.

From the perspective of one who has made this journey from conception to birth to newborn status, with all the learning that has taken place along the way, what do you understand as the main themes or story of your life? What do you believe or sense your life to be about?

Record your observations on these last questions.

When you have finished, stand up, move around, splash some water on your face—and then leave all your notes for a few days. At the end of this time come back to them and see what deeper information may be there for you.

For some people, the journey within this exercise offers so much insight into themselves that it becomes almost a reinvention of who they are, a rewriting of the story they have accepted and lived by up until this point in their lives. They see things in new ways as a result: they have a better understanding of their parents, the choices they had to make, and the ways they behaved. Finally, in some cases, they are able to let go and forgive the old hurts they have carried with them all their lives.

One of our participants, a forty-three-year-old woman, had a difficult childhood and still felt fearful, disempowered, and uncomfortable around others as a result of her early experiences. This is her account of the journey:

> Amazing. I gained a sense and feeling of love I have never really felt or witnessed between my parents. There was a loving passion that has in my lifetime only shown itself as anger and disagreement between them.
>
> Now I feel a greater understanding of my parents, my creation, and why I chose them. I understand more fully what fears, feelings, and dreams my parents had for me prior to my birth and can appreciate the stress my birth and babyhood placed on them. For the first time, I was able to experience the feeling of being created out of pure love and perfection.
>
> I felt a total sense of my power and strength as I was conceived and knew that it is all about pure love. Everything that happens after birth is imperfect because as humans we will never be perfect, but we can strive toward loving totally and unconditionally.

As Don Snyder puts it in *Of Time and Memory*, no matter what the stories of our lives, we can "hope that we are all preceded in this world by a love story." If we can see that in our parents, then something of our lives can also change and we can find "the path back through stars and memory."[1]

WHO ARE YOU?

What jailer is so inexorable as one's self?
NATHANIEL HAWTHORNE, *THE HOUSE OF THE SEVEN GABLES*

This seemingly simple process is, in some ways, an extension of the Conception Journey. All that is required of participants is that they sit in pairs, facing each other and making gentle physical contact. One person is elected questioner and the other respondent. The questioner's task is simply to ask the respondent, "Who are you?" The respondent's job is to answer the question honestly and from the heart each time it is put to him or her. Whenever the respondent runs out of steam during a particular answer, the questioner poses the same question. After thirty minutes, respondent and questioner swap roles.

This Zen-like practice is actually more difficult than it seems (if you do not have a partner, you may sit in front of a mirror with your eyes closed* and ask yourself, "Who are you?"). Initially, respondents tend to answer in terms of their many perceived social roles (as most of us habitually do in our daily conversations): "I am a doctor," "I am a mother," "I care for others," "I am a child," and so on.

After a few repetitions of the question, however, people soon begin to understand their participation in a more universal scheme: "I am a drop of water in an ocean," "I am a leaf in the breeze," "I am a grain of sand in a desert," and so on. This is closer to the "divine consciousness" of many spiritual or religious experiences and certainly closer to the effects of prolonged meditation and the theta states recorded in isolation experiments. Nevertheless, it still amounts to a labeling of experience and the acceptance of a role of some kind—that is, to identify ourselves with a drop of water or a leaf in the breeze is essentially no different from seeing ourselves as a doctor or a mother in that it still represents a limitation of the human spiritual experience, which may, in fact, be infinite. The more symbolic, metaphorical, or poetic nature of such responses does suggest, however, that participants are beginning to make the journey across the corpus callosum of the brain, moving from a rational and conditioned view of the world to a more holistic and intuitive understanding of it, and growing to see their greater potential.

The more remarkable change in the respondents, however, comes after

---

*It is useful to sit before a mirror even though your eyes are closed, as this gives a sense of "witness," a sense that "someone" is present there with you who requires an answer to your questions.

about twenty minutes into the exercise, when they begin to give responses such as "I don't know who I am" or (often in a surprised tone) "I am everything."

At our retreats, this realization is followed by a developing silence within the dark room and a change in the energy or atmosphere that feels like the arrival of a new presence. There is something of the numinous about it, like an agreement on the truth (or, at least, on *a* truth) has been reached between questioners and respondents. And, of course, in one sense, this is the experience of being human: we have no idea who we are! But rather than seeing this realization as a failing, we can view it as a triumph, for within it there is much power: It means we are free to be anyone and anything we choose—suddenly, we have freed ourselves from labels, whether "mother," "doctor," "ocean," or "leaf." This is the truth of understanding that begins to fill the darkness of the room.

As one participant explains it:

> I found it hard to stay in my body as I felt myself flowing off into many forms of who I was. I found it a very powerful experience, questioning my paradigms of self and being. From the point of view of asking the question ["Who are you?"], that too felt very powerful, as if holding a space for one's partner to truly look into themselves.

Another, Lisa, offers, "I was everything and nothing . . . anything I chose to be. I enjoyed listening to my partner and the feeling of closeness in sharing myself in this way with another. I risked more of myself."

The common conclusion that we reach by undertaking this exercise is that there is nothing to add or take away from our being, for it already contains its absolute essence beyond the realms of religious dogma, belief systems, and moral precepts.

A frequent phenomenon that also occurs during this exercise is that our identity in relation to gender melts away and we define ourselves in terms of "everything and nothing," as Lisa put it, rather than in terms of maleness or femaleness. This is much closer, in fact, to a tribal and natural perspective. The modern Western worldview is fundamentally different from native perceptions in that it is based on dualistic thinking (good/bad, right/wrong, and so forth). This perception extends to our understanding of gender: we are male or female.

Many protohistorical cultures have a very different point of view, however, one suggesting that gender is merely a social phenomenon arising from expectations for how a person of a given sex should behave. In older traditions, gender can be changed depending on the situation. For example, many Native American tribes have three, five, or seven genders. The Chukchi of Siberia recognize seven, as did the rabbis of the Talmud, who debated the status, responsibilities, and roles of each one. Within indigenous traditions it is not uncommon for there to be five sexes, seven genders,* and four hundred sexual orientations.

Traditionally, within these cultures "dual-sexed" people are viewed without stigma and, in fact, are regarded as emissaries of the Creator. They are treated with deference and respect, even considered sacred, for they are seen to embody both Mother Earth and Father Sky and to hold both a masculine and feminine heart within their souls. In consequence, they are thought to have twice the power of others in the group and often perform a special (typically, shamanic) role that is sanctioned by tribal mythology. The blind Greek sage Teiresias was considered especially wise, for example, because he had been changed into a woman for seven years and so knew the ways of both sexes. Such sages are "everything and nothing" too—"anything they choose to be."

Along with the opportunity to disregard gender labels, this exercise gives participants the chance to experiment with and explore their five senses. Actually, rather than five senses, which is the number, first ascribed by Aristotle, that we in our Western culture accept, in many indigenous cultures there are an indeterminate number that allows the boundaries of each sense to be blurred.

---

*In these traditions, the sex is generally—but not exclusively—expressed in terms of the physical and the gender in terms of the internal state.

Interestingly, the common consensus now within the scientific community is that there are at least twenty-one senses. If we are able to accomplish the small feat of closing our eyes, stretching out our arms, and standing on one leg, we obviously have our senses to thank. But which ones? Certainly sight, sound, taste, smell, or touch aren't involved.

What becomes clear within darkness is the fallacy of the idea that our sensations depend on which sensory organ picks up information. Our eyes do not just see, our ears do not just hear. . . . In fact, eyes may just as well hear and ears may just as well see. Indeed, the more we explore our sense organs, the more senses we appear to have and the more multifunctional all of these senses seem to become.

One phenomenon that often occurs among our participants, for example, is *synesthesia*, a blending and extension of the senses. The most commonly reported form is the experience of sounds as colors, which changes the nature of spoken words and the meanings behind them (as well as the experience of music and poetry) so that new levels of information are revealed. In the question "Who are you?" for example, participants often see the word *who* as green, *are* as red, and *you* with the question mark as white (without the question mark *you* is often experienced as light blue). When all the words are together, however, the sentence becomes orange. Try it for yourself and see what colors these words assume. Of course, tone of voice is also important. If the question is asked accusingly (meaning something akin to "Who do you think you are?"), participants offer that the sentence becomes red and the words appear sharp or jagged.

Participants also talk of the textures of particular aromas, of being able to hear a taste or feel a color. Some have even reported seeing with the tongue. Given the right set of circumstances, we likely all possess this cross-sense facility to a greater or lesser extent, which may shed light on why we say minor chords are sad, why the particular progression of chords in blues music is blue, and why lemons taste sharp.

The reports of synesthesia from our participants suggest that our usual understanding of what it is to sense something should be reevaluated. They also raise new questions, of course, about who we are and how limited—or limitless—are our creative imagination and our understanding of the world. Some of this also ties in to recent scientific research in what has come to be called "neuroplasticity."

As recently as the late 1980s the human brain was considered to be a sort of biological computer that, as one scientist put it, "secretes thoughts the way kidneys secrete urine." We now know that the brain is much more malleable and fluidly organized than this analogy to biological computing suggests, and that it changes with every perception and every action.

Over the past decade, for example, compelling evidence for neuroplasticity has come from studies of the blind by Alvaro Pascual-Leone, a professor at Harvard University. In the early 1990s Pascual-Leone and his colleagues at the National Institutes of Health showed that, as blind adults learned to read Braille, the region of the somatosensory (touch-sensitive) cortex responding to input from the reading finger greatly enlarged. The brain was physically adapting itself to a new way of "seeing."[2]

In 1996 the researchers made an even more startling discovery: input from the sensitized finger was lighting up not only the somatosensory cortex on the side of the brain, but parts of the *visual* cortex near the back of the brain as well.

Could it be that, in adult blind people, new nerve connections were reaching out across the brain to occupy neural "real estate" left vacant by the lack of input from their sightless eyes? Pascual-Leone tested that notion by doing just what we do within the Darkness Visible work: putting sighted people into darkness for periods of five days.

After as little as two days, however, MRI scans were showing bursts of activity in the visual cortex when subjects performed tasks with their fingers, or even when they listened to tunes or words. This was far too short a time for new nerve connections to grow from the touch and hearing regions of the cortex to the area processing sight, of course, and a few hours after the subjects were removed from darkness the visual cortex again responded only to input from the eyes. The research, nonetheless, is intriguing and raises all sorts of questions about what it is that accounts for this sudden ability of the brain to "see" with input not from the eyes but from fingers and ears.

Pascual-Leone further suggests that the connections from these senses to the visual cortex may already be there for every one of us, but remain unused as long as the eyes are doing their job. When the eyes of the shaman and the explorers of darkness are shut down, however, the brain is programmed to seek the next best way for the body to receive necessary information from the environment. The conclusion is that the brain may not be organized into sensory modalities at all, and that which science has called the visual cortex for the past century may well not be devoted exclusively to the eyes. We can, in fact, "see" with every sense.

Several other studies support this conclusion. A study of blind individuals performed at the Beth Israel Deaconess Medical Center of Harvard Medical School showed brain reorganization and behavioral compensations following sensory deprivation, with clear neuroplastic changes, most striking of which was the activation of the occipital cortex in response to auditory and tactile stimulation. Put simply, the brain compensates for even temporary blindness by allowing people to "see" with their other senses.[3]

Another study has shown that, although Absolute Pitch (AP) is typically possessed by less than 20 percent of all musicians, in a sample of forty-six blind subjects (less than half of whom had any musical training), 57 percent were capable of AP, suggesting the development through blindness of different neural mechanisms.[4]

A third study shows that visual deprivation may lead to enhanced performance of the other senses—for example, that sighted individuals blindfolded for five days perform better than ordinarily sighted subjects in Braille discrimination tasks, irrespective of tactile training. These results suggest that visual deprivation speeds up Braille learning and "may be associated with behaviorally relevant neuroplastic changes."[5]

Yet another study compares PET (positron emission tomography) scans of Braille readers blinded early in life with scans of sighted subjects. The study reports that, when both types of subjects are given a Braille-reading task, different areas of the brain are used and, significantly, that in blind people, tactile processing pathways are rerouted to brain regions originally reserved for visual shape discrimination.[6] An earlier study published by many of the same researchers had already shown that in blind subjects cortical areas normally reserved for vision may be activated by the other senses.[7]

These findings are quite consistent with our observations on Darkness Visible retreats—that when people are unsighted their hands become their eyes and the sensitivity of their fingertips increases as, hands outstretched in front of them while walking, these become their main means of negotiating the terrain ahead. (As Jez commented, "The only things that remained were my hands. These became my eyes and my fingertips became extremely sensitive, as if I was really seeing with them.")

Perhaps it is not just the hands that are capable of such increased sensitivity, in fact, but the entire body. Colin Wilson, in his book *Mysteries* (New York: Perigee, 1980), reports on a blind Russian girl who is able to read out loud and quite accurately from a normally typeset book by simply laying it flat on her stomach. If sighted people can develop expertise in Braille after just five days in darkness, why might similar neuroplastic changes and enhanced sensitivity not be possible across the entire body after more prolonged spells of darkness?

EARTH'S EMBRACE

And I will dress you in clay and have you eat earth,
So that you can savor the womb of this world.

GIOCONDA BELLI, "TELL ME"

There is one experience in our darkness work that closely resembles the isolation-tank experience referred to in chapter 4: the burial of participants overnight as a deepening of darkness.

Going into the darkness underground is very different from being unsighted above the ground. Above ground, we are in the terrestrial realm and our minds may drift to notions of the heavens. But underground, within the earth, below its surface and surrounded by matter, we are rooted and at the same time afloat in a womb of potential, for every birth—the first and most momentous journey—begins in darkness.

The womb of the earth is a microcosm of the world. It is the primal stage, the original theater. Within the Path of Pollen, the practice of live burial is referred to as earth's embrace. But burial is actually a cross-cultural initiatory practice for many tribal people because it allows the initiate to receive nurturing and guidance from the earth itself. The practice forms part of the male puberty rites for the Dagara peoples of Africa, for example, and assists them in their initiatory transformations. It can also be found within the Curanderismo tradition of Central America, in which the ceremony is often offered to women who have been raped or sexually abused. Burial in volcanic sand is also a part of the healing practices of the psychic surgeons of the Philippines, who use it to stimulate the body's recuperative powers. It is known in Buddhism in the form of the tantric encounters with death undertaken in Thailand. In India, most famously of all, there is a long spiritual history of meditative entombment within the earth and in caves. One Indian mystic, Ramaswamy, claimed to have been buried in this way for one hundred years. When his tomb was finally discovered accidentally, he emerged from his timeless sleep to continue in holy service.

Depending on how it is undertaken and the intention behind it, the ceremonial event of meditative entombment can mean many different things—sometimes all at once: a blessing, a healing, a letting go of the past, the acceptance of a new future, a celebration of life, or a potent form of vision quest that helps those who undertake it to find greater clarity in life. It can also be a rehearsal of our deaths, and it is this aspect that can be the most enlightening, for experiencing a smaller death in the dark womb of the earth can give greater meaning and value to life and to the light when, in the morning, we are born again from our graves.

On our retreats, participants enter not simply a grave, but rather a vehicle, an "earth ship" that allows them to sail the stars within and outside of themselves, on a voyage of self-discovery and exploration of who they are or could become. Still wearing Mindfolds, they lie down in the earth alone at a depth of about three feet. The opening to the earth is covered in sticks and twigs over which a tarpaulin is placed. The soil that they had previously removed from their tombs is then placed over the top and an airhole is created, allowing them plentiful oxygen for the work ahead. Participants remain in total darkness, alone throughout the night, while we watch over their circle of graves.

Not surprisingly, it is this complete immersion—submersion—in darkness that can have the most profound effects, which have included the healing of birth traumas and liberation from unhealthy life events—all delivered in images, mythology, and metaphor by the experience itself, without any need for therapeutic intervention.

The following account is in many ways typical of what can happen to people when they enter total darkness within the earth, without even the light of the moon upon their skins.

I heard the sound of earth being thrown on nearby graves and that felt scary—reminding me that I too was in the ground. I wanted reassurance that if I called out I would be heard and would have support. This was important to me, as I never ask for help and usually do things alone. Receiving support was an important part of my journey as I didn't believe in people's ability to offer me help when I needed it.

[At one point during the night] I got really angry and started swearing and shouting at the earth. I kicked and screamed and hit the walls and threw a fit, crying all the time, angry and upset.

After what felt like a huge emotional and physical release, I calmed down and started relaxing into the darkness. I went deeper and deeper and saw all sorts of strange things in the dark. I started to tell the earth why I was there and talked about myself, but I felt like I was lost and wasn't being heard. I had trouble breathing and was taking big gulps—breathing very hard—but my chest sounded like it was wheezing and I couldn't get my breath. (I don't suffer with any breathing difficulties usually.) I could hear the sound of my breath deafening me; this scared me. I tried for ages to control my breathing and to calm down.

[Eventually I called out. Simon came and] I told him how I was angry at Mother Earth. He told me this was okay; she would support me and I could tell her everything about me. This made sense and really helped me focus again.

I curled up and molded my body into the earth. I spoke to the walls quietly and told all. I told my story and how I felt, what had happened in my life—the sexual abuse, the violence, what it was like to grow up in my family, how I felt about this, and my fears and my hopes and dreams, the despair, my anger at not being able to do anything right, not being able to fit in. It all came out and I talked and cried until I could talk no more and was exhausted. It felt good and I did feel calm and supported and held by the earth.

Then I made a commitment to Mother Earth—it was about my quest to find the child within. I needed to fetch that little girl back and to make a decision about how I could deal with my family and how I could remain on my path. I asked Mother Earth for help and told her I was leaving all the crap behind and moving on with my life.

I wanted to go further, deeper into the darkness, but felt that I needed to rest before doing this. Then, as I was lying there, Ross told me it was morning and time to rise from the grave. I didn't believe it, as it seemed like hardly any time had passed since I had been in there. I didn't want to come out—I wasn't nearly ready. I really couldn't believe I had been in the grave all night, as time just seemed to have stopped while [I was] in there.

I asked Simon what time I had called out for help. He said about 3:15 or 3: 30 A.M. This was significant because I was actually born at 3:15 A.M.—and as I was struggling to breathe in the grave I felt like I was fighting for my life . . . maybe like being born?

Another participant's experience was in some ways similar, although different in its emotional impact:

> This was such an exquisite and sublimely sensual experience for me. Upon entering the grave I felt as if I had slipped into the depths of the earth and had a remarkable sense of space above me, as if I were entombed in some high-vaulted temple. I chanted and toned and heard many overtones. When I stopped making sound myself, I heard words and sounds emerge spontaneously from the earth.
>
> [It] was also an intense physical experience. My body was as an antenna for the myriad vibrations of the earth, from beneath which emerged a "heartbeat," a regular, deep, rhythmic vibration that seemed to come from the core of the planet. I was aware of engaging and disengaging with the flow, at times moving my body, and I found myself wondering if I was truly sailing away, only to stumble upon the realization that I had already arrived and this was it!
>
> As the night progressed and I deepened into the work, I found my body temperature rising and I became so hot that I removed the layers between myself and the earth to be in my natural form in the arms of my true Mother. This was an experience of unconditional love, total acceptance, and deep trust such as I have never known and would not have imagined possible. I felt deeply humble and yet incredibly powerful, as if truly knowing and owning my authentic self for the first time. [This authenticity] was my gift to my Mother the Earth, in thanks for the beauty of the life I have.

After participants have emerged from their earth ships, refilled their graves, and rested from their night of work within the ground, we gather together once more and ask them to recount their experiences of the Conception Journey (pages 94–97) and of their time in the womb of Mother Earth in order to see if there are parallels between the two.

Invariably, there are. This is an extract from a letter written by a 2004 participant in the Darkness Visible retreat:

> You asked that we put our conception and burial side by side to see if there are any correspondences. . . . I had one huge correspondence and it was [about] "digestion.". . .
>
> It started with the conception journey, at the point where my mother first feeds me. I did not need to be fed; I was not hungry but just wanted to bask in the love of my parents. However, my mother needed to feed me and I responded to her needs by allowing myself to be fed. . . .
>
> Early in my burial, I had a birthing experience in which I strained to give birth. I feel I let go quite a lot of pain there. . . . I stretched my body in new ways, snarled and screamed . . . and ate. In the end I felt like I had been liberated.
>
> Rather than trying to digest my experiences, I am now allowing my Self to be digested.

What is interesting is that, in her experience of the Conception Journey, this participant realizes that in some way she allowed her mother to take power from her when she went along with her mother's desire to feed her even though she herself did not want to be fed. In the birthing experience during the burial, she was clearly more in her own power and chose to eat because she wanted to eat. Shamans would call this a power retrieval, in which we get back the energy we have given away to others and start to live our own lives by our own choices. And, as this participant says, in such circumstances it is better not to rationalize or undermine the experience (by attempting to "digest" it) but to allow ourselves "to be digested"—to experience it fully so that a new life story can emerge.

The burial story of another participant is also interesting in this respect:

My whole sense of reality has altered. I now believe that there are other dimensions; I have suspended my judgment about what reality is and, by doing so, can see much more of the world.

Life has become more exciting and I feel more connected to the world than I have ever felt before. I feel more confident in many ways, and in my ability to express myself from my heart without qualifying or judging what I think or feel.

I am learning how to love and be loved. I am allowing feelings of excitement, adventure, passion into my life and opening myself up to trusting people in a different way. Feelings of the joy of being in the present and hope for the future have been rekindled, and a thirst for knowledge has been reawakened in me. I feel like I am a child all over again.

A rebirth, we might say.

TRY THIS

Your Conception/Life Story

And this is the simple truth: that to live is to feel oneself lost. He who accepts it has already begun to find himself. . . . The only genuine ideas [are] the ideas of the shipwrecked. All the rest is rhetoric, posturing, farce.
SOREN KIERKEGAARD, *THE JOURNALS OF SOREN KIERKEGAARD*

Each of us has life stories partly written for us by the authors of our lives: our parents. Like any story, however, we are free to change the beginning, middle, and end, or to rewrite the plot if we wish. In fact, in some ways it may even be our duty to do so.

As Sam Keen writes:

The task of any individual who wants to be free is to demythologise and demystify the authority or myth that has unconsciously informed his or her life. We gain personal authority and find our unique sense of self only when we learn to distinguish between our own story—our autobiographical truths—and the official myths that have previously governed our minds, feelings, and actions.

This begins when we ask: "What story have I been living? What myth has captivated me?" It ends only when we tell our own story, and authorise our own life rather than accept the official view of things.[8]

Close your eyes and imagine your life is literally a story and you are its hero. What sort of a story is it? What is taking place in it?

Still with eyes closed, write down a synopsis of the story that emerges, including the plot line, characters, and dramas that take form. Don't veto anything; just write what you see. It doesn't matter how untidy it looks on the page.

It is said that all good stories center around a problem or a challenge for the hero and its resolution. This is our mythic quest. Open your eyes and read your story. What themes emerge? What are the problems, challenges, and possible solutions? How do the characters act? How does the plot twist and turn? Where are the big, dramatic set pieces and how do they tie in to the plot or relate to the characters involved?

This is your life story—how you see it and how you see yourself. Embellish it as much as you wish or rewrite it entirely if you like. Solve the problems it poses and sprinkle it with adventures and happiness. Then—just for today—try living as if your happy ending were already a reality.

Who Are You?

Mystics and sages tell us that we live in a world of projection—that there are no other characters in our stories, only the selves we project. So, who are you?

Choose a character from your life story in "Your Conception/Life

Story"—from the first version, before you embellished or rewrote it. With your eyes closed, answer the question "Who are you?" from this character's perspective, speaking his or her words out loud.

Pay attention to the character's feelings, and yours, and any images that come to mind as you and the character answer the question a few times. See how these images change. What does this tell you about who you are and where you might be going?

Earth's Embrace

It is possible to get a sense of the burial experience without actually burying yourself by finding a quiet place in nature, such as a cave, a hollow in the land, or a grove of trees, and entering the darkness there. One effect of this is that you may get a feeling of connection to something much greater than yourself: the energy of the earth. Find such a spot. When you settle there, close your eyes. How does the natural darkness around you begin to change your awareness? Do you feel a sense of expanding connection?

Ask any questions you have in mind and note how the earth answers you.

What's Your Name, What's Your Number?

The Question of Identity

The principal ritual in most puberty and initiation rites is a death
and resurrection ritual in which your name is changed. You die to
the name you had and are resurrected with a new identity.

JOSEPH CAMPBELL, *REFLECTIONS ON THE ART OF LIVING*

A FURTHER SERIES of exercises in Darkness Visible retreats builds upon the deep questioning of self—Who are we? Where do we fit into the world?—that is invoked by the journey into darkness. One of these exercises consists of further stripping participants of their usual identities through the removal of their names, which are replaced with numbers.

This might seem disturbing on some level. The removal of our names is, after all, associated with a complete loss of self and an accompanying loss of freedom. After all, many "total institutions" (to use the term invented by the sociologist Erving Goffman to describe all-encompassing ideologies) use the same practice, and most of these institutions have negative connotations: prisons, POW camps, the military, asylums, hospitals, and sometimes cults give their members numbers instead of names. But so do less threatening institutions, such as airlines and credit card companies. Indeed, so does the government itself. In fact, the first real social identity for most of us consists of our birth certificate and a social security number.

The point is that our names and our numbers are primary sources of identity for all of us, and someone—that is, someone other than our-selves—has given both of them to us. The purpose of our exercise is not to create a new total institution for participants or induct people into a cult, but rather to allow them to explore the aspects of their identities that have been imposed on them by others and that have now become so accepted that they typically go unquestioned.

This exercise, therefore, is not an induction into the membership of any belief system or way of being; it is instead an opportunity for us to realize and think about the memberships we already have.

TAKING AWAY THE GIVEN NAME

I'm going to memorize your name and throw my head away.

OSCAR LEVANT

On day one of the exercise, each participant is given a number. This is done in a totally nonlinear way that actually borders on the comic in order to demonstrate subtly the ludicrous nature of trying to reduce a human being to a series of digits that ultimately, in the case of the government, can be stored on a computer.

Participants sit in circle and as they are touched, one by one, they are assigned numbers in completely random fashion: the first person may be 1, the next 763, the next 48, and so on. Participants are then told that they are to refer to one another by these numbers. Either they agree (as they most often do) or they rebel: they may object to the imposition of these numbers and insist on continuing to use their original names—which, of course, have also been imposed on them by others! Each response will take the workshop in a different direction. Normally, however, there is no such rebellion, and some participants even find their new number comforting.

One participant remarks:

> I enjoyed giving away my name and being known by a number. It gave me a new sense of identity that was full of potential and possibilities. I enjoyed others' referring to me by my number, too. I also had fun wondering about the meaning of the number, and although I didn't come up with any definite meaning, this was okay with me.
>
> Being a number made me feel a part of everything and equal in some sense because I was able to shed my past history and start out fresh.

Another participant saw the exercise as "intriguing" and comments upon her feeling of "speculation and needing to attach meaning to our respective numbers." Once again, there is no meaning to these numbers— they are assigned completely at random—but her comment does illustrate the importance, often unconscious, that we ascribe to these sources of our identity. We buy into our names and numbers, and this attempt to find meaning in an identification that is meaningless ultimately describes— and limits—our sense of who we are.

As if to underline this, on day two of the exercise, participants are stripped of their numbers and are given "proper" names. These are not what is expected, however. After a dramatic buildup during which we praise the human spirit and declare that human beings can never be reduced to numbers, we move among the participants and whisper to them their new ritual names, which we have received "from the spirit world." Each listens excitedly, then they all stand in a circle and announce their new names to the group:

"I am Washing Machine!"

"I am New York Herald Tribune!"

"I am Yeah Yeah Go Yankees Go!"

More complete nonsense. The point, once again, is to demonstrate our attachments to, and sometimes our need for, labels and definitions of ourselves. By day two, participants are beginning to get the point and to see the humor behind it: "Further intrigue and great amusement. Something is going on here but I haven't a clue what it is—or have I?" "This too was fun. . . . I felt like I had progressed a little and liked my new name—Pipe. I enjoyed the image and played around with meanings in my mind."

On day three, we take a different approach. Participants are invited to choose a name for themselves and let go of the previous identities that we (and, by association, others) have imposed on them. The point is to illustrate that we can be anything or anyone we want to be. This is in keeping with Joseph Campbell's comment that, as part of the initiatory cycle, "you die to the name you had and are resurrected with a new identity."[1]

Although this identity exercise is treated in a lighthearted way, the power of names and naming is shown here in that some participants find choosing their own name the hardest part. It is not the imposition of an identity that frightens them, but rather the realization of the underlying freedom and power they have to forge their own sense of self. To us, this is reminiscent of the words of Marianne Williamson, used by Nelson Mandela during his inauguration speech: "Our deepest fear is not that we are inadequate. Our deepest fear is that we are powerful beyond measure. It is our light, not our darkness, that most frightens us."

> Being asked to choose my own name felt good but also scary because I thought that people would make associations with [it] and might start judging me by the name I had chosen. This was more difficult for me than being given a number or an object name.
>
> I felt good about the name I chose for myself, though—Kyte—because of what this represents for me: freedom, flying, playing, soaring, being a child, flowing, and reaching for the sky and testing the boundaries while remaining held by a thread [to] the ground.
>
> I found it empowering and oddly quite charming. I felt a softness flow through the group and a sense of us hearing each other in a new way.

Finally, near the end of the course, participants return to their original names, the ones given them by their parents. But they rarely go back to who they were; the journey of this exercise has taken them to a new understanding of their identity and what these labels have meant for them. They can now look at their original names in a fresh way; they have been freed from some of their associations and are able to resurrect and reinvent themselves.

> [This felt like] coming full circle, completion and grounding of the work into our realities—even though for me this bears no resemblance to my previous reality.

> Returning to my own name was like a gateway. . . . I felt a sense of having moved forward and reclaimed part of my identity alongside the new parts of me I had experienced throughout the course. I felt stronger and more powerful and had a sense of being part of and attached to something much bigger than just me.

> *Since the world is an unsolvable mystery whose surface has scarcely*
> *been penetrated by our efforts to know and explain, the assumption*
> *that we can understand . . . is actually a symptom of insecurity*
> *and an inability to tolerate ambiguity and darkness. Nothing is*
> *less appropriate in our time than the posture of certainty.*
>
> SAM KEEN, *FIRE IN THE BELLY*

MEETING THE ANCESTORS

It is not just our name that connect us to our lineage and give us our identity; it is our entire family history. Our ancestors, though many of them have been long dead, continue to play a significant part in our life. The fact that we were born, for example, in one country and not another; that we have been raised as part of a certain culture and lifestyle; that particular talents, life stories, or patterns recur in our family; that our family may have secrets and "ghosts in the closet"—these are all matters that are the affairs of our ancestors, not of our own making, but they still play their roles in the mythology of our life.

The story of one woman, Eli, illustrates this. When Eli became pregnant, she entered therapy to deal with family issues because she wanted to lay to rest the ghosts of her own unhappy childhood. But because her childhood patterns were so fixed in her psyche, she merely ended up unthinkingly dragging her own past into the future of her family.*

Eli was from a broken home. Her father had left almost as soon as she was born and she was raised by her mother, an insecure woman who, according to Eli, had hidden her fears behind alcoholism and drug use, parties and pretense. (She invented an English degree from Oxford University, for example, in the hope that her peers and children would like and respect her for her accomplishments.) Eli had grown up in this atmosphere and now wanted a stable family of her own as a consequence of this falseness and insecurity.

When she became an adult, though, despite her apparent desire for stability and honesty, Eli embarked on a series of confused and unsatisfying relationships, just like her mother. When an unplanned pregnancy arose, Eli kept the baby but left her boyfriend (breaking up the family, as her father had left her when she was born). She met another man and four unwanted pregnancies followed in almost as many months, all of which she terminated without telling the father-to-be, despite her alleged need for honesty within her relationships. She then left that lover, too.

Now she was pregnant again by another man. She went into therapy because she and her new partner were having difficulties in their relationship, which came as no surprise, given her background. This time, she said she wanted to resolve her issues before their baby was born.

Even though Eli was fully aware of her problems, the therapy failed. A few weeks of therapy, after all, cannot repair years of living out a pattern of family dramas and half-spoken truths. Almost inevitably, Eli left her new

---

*A fuller examination of this particular life drama, along with more information on ancestral healing work, appears in the book *The Spiritual Practices of the Ninja* by Ross Heaven.

partner. She then moved away, taking their new son with her and giving her lover no forwarding address.

Effectively, Eli made her lover the "abandoning father" to mirror her own father while she, in turn, became her own mother—a single parent with a new orphan son to bring up in the same way she had been raised, with all the attendant dramas and pretense. This was her family curse, so to speak, and the one she also imposed on her son.

"The boy has to disengage himself from his mother, get his energy into himself, and then start forth. That's what the myth of 'Young man, go find your father' is all about," says Joseph Campbell.[2] Eli had been denied a father and then, in turn, denied her son one. In so doing, she had effectively set up his life drama for him: to find the father his mother had stolen from him. The fact that this was so like Eli's own drama may explain why she felt so compelled to take ownership of her son: by controlling him, she could ensure that at least this one man (her son) would stay with her.

There is always a "first event" in family dramas such as these. We've looked at the life that Eli unconsciously engineered for her son, tracing it back to events in her own drama. No doubt Eli's mother and father were not acting in isolation either, and there were games between them and their parents that made their own lives of distance and drama more likely. And so it goes, down the family line.

During Darkness Visible workshops, participants have an opportunity to explore this family history and to find the first event that caused the wound in their ancestral line that has contributed to their current identity. Often, they are able to identify the family curse of which they feel themselves to be a part.

Participants are guided on a visualization to meet with an ancestor at the point in their family history when this curse first arose. They are then able to "intervene" in this history in order to release the burdens of the past and free themselves from hindering aspects of their life story.

We include this exercise here so you can undertake the same journey, if you wish. Read the visualization first, then relax, close your eyes, and allow your imagination to take you where it will.

ANCESTOR VISUALIZATION

Everything that has ever been is a circle. The moon is a circle, the sun is a circle, as is the earth; the cycle of the day, the changing of the seasons, the journey of a man and a woman's life—all of these are circles.

Time is no different. It is not linear or progressive; it does not move forward without reaching back. We carry our past with us into our present and from these we create our future—which may be much like our past if we do not break the circle.

First, close your eyes. In your mind's eye, see yourself standing in a place of nature, somewhere that connects you with the earth. Really feel this place: the sun on your face, the wind in your hair, the ground beneath your feet. With you is a witness, an aspect of your deeper self who is there to record what you see and hear and feel and sense. The witness understands the symbols—the metaphor and the myth—in what you see. He or she asks the deeper questions and records the answers for you.

The witness asks now, for example, about the meaning of this landscape around you. Why is it a desert or a rainforest, a harrowed field or a cold mountain peak? What is the meaning, the symbolism, the metaphor for you in this particular landscape, when you could have chosen any place on Earth? Don't trouble yourself with searching for the answer now. The witness knows the answer to this question and will reveal it to you in time.

In this landscape, however you perceive it, there is a doorway that can take you into a past that you know, somewhere within you, and have always known. How does this doorway look? Is it huge and oak and locked? Is it a white gate, partly open, in a picket fence? Is it featureless or carved with symbols? The witness observes and knows why your doorway appears as it does.

Open the doorway and step through. As you do so, find yourself in another world: a world of magical possibilities, where choices were once made in your family's past and can be remade, if you wish.

As you explore this world with your eyes, notice that someone is walking toward you—someone who looks a bit like you. This is the ancestor you have come here to meet, the person in your family's history who once made a choice and, by that choice, created ripples in the universe that have led down through the ages and through your family line, in some mysterious way, to the person you are today.

Which of your ancestors appears to you? Is it someone you know, a relative from your recent past, or is he or she from a time more distant? Or is this person more an archetypal energy representing a pattern in your family that you have noticed across the generations?

Welcome this ancestor and tell him or her why you are here: to ask for help in understanding your life by seeing the choices this person made, the actions he or she took, and the reasons behind them. Ask to see the gifts this ancestor has bestowed on you, as well as the patterns that, through his or her choices, have become burdens down through the generations. Make a connection with this ancestor, this spirit who loves you and who was once simply human, simply trying to do what was best for him- or herself, for his or her children—for you, no matter what the outcome (perhaps unintended) of these choices.

Thank your ancestor for his or her gifts that have helped you and that continue to serve you, and then ask what you can do to release those other energies you perceive to be unhelpful so that you can let go of these attachments. Perhaps your ancestor asks for a healing, or to perform a releasing ritual of some kind. Be guided by your intuition as to how you best can help. Remember that the witness stands with you in this and that he or she is a master of symbol and metaphor. Call on this being for assistance if you need it.

When you are ready, thank your ancestor for helping you on this quest for understanding, and offer your love in return, knowing you can always return here. As you turn to leave, your ancestor calls the witness forward and whispers something to him or her that you cannot hear. And then, more audibly, your ancestor speaks these words: *"Do not let my descendant forget what I have just told you."* The witness nods in understanding and then returns to you.

Make your way together back through the doorway behind you, toward the landscape you first entered. Speak with the witness, who has observed and recorded all and who has other information for you about the things you have seen, the symbols beneath them, the myths and the metaphors, the mystery and the magic of your life. What are these? What are the words you are never to forget, the ones your ancestor offered you from the perspective of someone who has lived life and made choices? Listen to what the witness has to say.

Then, knowing you can return to the witness at any time to discover more and to follow this conversation further, say farewell to him or her and turn around so that you see this room [the room in which you began the exercise], this circle of people within it [any of those who might be practicing this visualization along with you], and your body, here and now in the present of this physical reality—which may be a very different reality from what it was before, now that this healing work is done.

Come back to your body and to normal consciousness, feeling awake, aware, refreshed, and empowered to be exactly who you now are.

In our workshops after this exercise, we offer two gifts—a stick and a seed—to participants to help them with a ritual they will devise to break their ties to unhelpful events and energies from their past. We give them no instruction on how these might be used, but a typical response is to snap the stick in half, representing an end to the chain of negativity from their family history, and to plant the seed in the retreat center grounds so that something beautiful can grow from their commitment to a new and empowered future for themselves and their children.

Again, despite the apparent simplicity of the exercise, it is extremely powerful, and surprising information can often be revealed:

> The ancestral work was a revelation . . . a great thing to do for one's
> family. When I got home, I spent several days journeying to my
> ancestors to find out what state they were in and, if possible, help

sort them out. That proved very powerful, not to mention releasing for me and them. It sorted out a lot of bad energy.

Some astounding insights [arose] that have been deeply directive in the work I have done since. . . . I sensed a profound and deeply felt shift in the group energy after this work.

[It] tore me apart; emotion in free flow. Oh, the pain! Wonderful!

The ancestral work was amazing. I had very vivid visions of my ancestors. My Welsh and Irish ancestors were being violent and treating women badly. There were wars and fighting [and] extreme harshness where life was very difficult for men and women. The main issues that came to my attention were a lack of love and care of the children.

I was given the opportunity to talk to both sides, male and female, and offered the gift of my love to the ancestors in order to break [the] pattern. I told the ancestors how sad and painful it is to grow up where emotions are suppressed by drink and only anger, rage, and violence are allowed to be shown, where children do not feel loved or cared about and women are not respected. I told them how we now have a new generation of young children growing up and that this needs to change.

Two figures emerged and spoke to each other. They vanished and a white flower opened and a dove appeared. The message I received was one of peace and growth.

This was my most memorable and powerful exercise . . . the first time I truly, clearly, and deeply saw my ancestors, starting with my father and then his father. I connected, healed, and helped them.

I was truly thrown out of my normal life. I felt that all in the group had their own powerful experiences and became more profoundly aware of their actions in life.

This work for me related to the fact that there is a tradition of healing in my family on my mother's side. In my visions I met Ellie, a woman ostracized by society and her village for practicing witchcraft. She was a genuine, cunning woman and her spirit or divine spark led me to an underground chamber. A huge well was there and we both drank.

She asked me to release Ellie, the part of her that had suffered abuse and abject poverty and loneliness. We went to her cottage and there she was, dirtied and in squalor. I offered her release and she came to me. I broke into sobs and tears.

I realized that I had been carrying her hurt and unconsciously acting out her pain in my own life, especially during my teens and twenties—living in squalor, impoverished and marginalized by mainstream society because of my interest in magic and alternative spirituality—yet people were at the same time drawn to me for healing.

I've been working on these issues of my place in and contribution to society for a number of years from a different perspective, and I've left behind a lot of the pain and negativity that I've been carrying in early adulthood. However, I'd never guessed [at] the existence of Ellie [within me].

The work done here felt like a completion, a closing, a final resolution of those issues. It was a great honor to be the one chosen to reach back through the ages and release Ellie's soul. She is an honored ancestor reclaimed.

ENTERING THE TEMPLE OF PEACE: ASKLEPIAN DREAM INCUBATION

It is well known that dreaming practices have been central to perennial and shamanic wisdom traditions the world over. However, many people associate these practices with traditions based outside of Europe, in particular with those in Mexico and Central America.

What is less well known is that European traditions of dreaming have been equally well established and reached a peak within the Greek mystery schools that developed the healing practice of Asklepian dream incubation, which was active for almost two millennia. In fact, incubation temples existed in various parts of Europe outside of Greece as well, including Britain, and these British temples may well have been used for a continuation of earlier Keltic rites.

Perhaps the greatest exponent of incubation dreaming methods was Pythagoras. Behind his philosophy was an awareness that the sun rises from the dark underworld, its home, and returns there every night. Thus, the source of greatest light is the darkness.

It was for this reason that many followers of Pythagoras built their own homes near volcanoes. The volcano was a channel for light from the depths of the darkness, a path for the fire that illuminated the earth and the heavens, with the sun and moon and stars mere reflections of this great flame from the underworld. Applying this principle to the mind, Pythagoras believed that in order to find clarity we must all enter darkness, physically as well as metaphorically, for darkness is the real source of light.

When he left the island of Samos, Pythagoras took with him the traditions and techniques of dream incubation as a means of exploring this illumined inner darkness. At his new home in Italy he built an underground chamber, where he would sit for extended periods in silent contemplation, returning from this dark underworld temple, he said, as a messenger of the gods.

A further example of oneiric (or dream) work from Europe, which may have been influenced by the Greek mystery schools, is found in the practices of medieval witch cults, as evidenced by records of some of the earliest witch trials in Toulouse. It was here in 1335 that the witch Catherine Delort affirmed that she visited the sabbat (or witches' midnight assembly) in her sleep, using a special dreaming state both to diminish the hold of profane perceptual conditioning and to take flight to the otherworld of uncommon reality.

Shamanic dreaming practices such as these awaken a separate reality within us, giving us controlled awareness of our dream life, a liberation of perception, and opportunities for receiving considerable wisdom and healing.

The original Greek temples were known as Asklepia—that is, dedicated to the healing god Asklepios. Considered to be places offering natural healing, they were usually associated with mineral springs and with large snakes kept in pits, undoubtedly a reference to the staff or wand carried by Asklepios—the caduceus— which features two intertwined snakes rising up a central staff.

The main Asklepian temple, near Chora, on the isle of Cos, was said to have been under the gaze of a famous statue of Aphrodite. The dream incubation chambers there eventually occupied three terraces tucked attractively into the fold of a limestone hill. The air in these temples was filled with the scent of flowers and the aroma of frankincense, eucalyptus, and citrus, the priests and healers understanding that our olfactory sense is the strongest of all (many of us can remember smells from twenty or thirty years ago) and that these beautiful aromas anchored the patient to the healing that took place.

As for the practice of incubation itself, after undergoing ritual purification and offering sacrifices to the local deities, individuals would spend a night within an incubation chamber, the *enkoimesis*, "sleeping in the sanctuary." If the gods willed it (and it seems they usually did), the patient received a dream, typically involving the appearance of the healer Asklepios, one of his priestesses, or one of his family, including snakes and dogs. The dream itself was usually enough to effect the cure. The "right" dream was the one that healed.

Dreams were interpreted by a *therapute* (the origin of our word *therapist*), who made a diagnosis based on the content and symbolic imagery of the patient's dream. While this sounds similar to modern-day psychoanalysis, this dream analysis was typically more focused on curing sicknesses of body or spirit than on psychological problem-solving. The key difference between classical and modern dream analysis was the sincere belief on the part of the ancients that such dreams emanated specifically from the deities and were healing in themselves.

This approach has, however, stood the test of time. Sigmund Freud and his one-time student Carl Jung both encouraged their patients to recount their dreams and use visualization as a route into their unconscious and the healing powers it contained. Freud called dreams the "royal road" to the unconscious and Jung himself spent many years exploring his inner world through the practice of active imagination. "The years when I was pursuing my inner images were the most important in my life," he later wrote. "In them, everything essential was decided."[3]

The success of such visualization stems from the fact that everything— good health or disease, a happy or an unhappy childhood—must first be imagined before it can be created. What we imagine—images—are our reality before this reality becomes visible to others or, often, to ourselves. What we see in our mind determines who we perceive ourselves to be and who we present to the world. Our subsequent interactions with others determine the quality of our lives. But it is our imaginings and ideas of self that come first. "Imagination is the beginning of creation," said George Bernard Shaw. "You imagine what you desire; you will what you imagine; and at last you create what you will."[4]

Because all things originate in the imagination, the image we have of ourselves and our circumstances is also key to our experience and understanding of life—whether we see life as something to be feared or enjoyed and ourselves as filled with potential or pain. Because of this, the purposeful use of images has a power that can be used to remodel— re-envision—our lives, to solve problems, and to deal with issues that are unresolved and, perhaps, not even a conscious part of our lives. By using our images in a constructive way, we gain access to greater personal freedom.

Everyone can work with images. If you relax and close your eyes right now and think about a situation you know, an image of that situation will come to mind. It may present itself as a feeling, a smell, a sense, or a picture of the scene. It may not be what you expect or even a replica of the scene itself but, however it is presented, it will be an accurate reflection of how you feel (or, rather, your unconscious feels) about that situation.

If you choose to contemplate a situation as simple as your drive to work, for example, you may not see yourself in your usual car or on the route you take each day—which would be the literal view of your journey. Instead, you might see, unasked for and unintended but bubbling up from your unconscious nonetheless, the image of a pit of vipers, or a monster truck driven by a demented monkey in the lane next to yours. Normally, you might be irritated at such an intrusive image that prevents you from doing what you are trying to do—that is, thinking about your drive to work. But in actuality this image is giving you powerful information about how you feel about your drive to work, which you can use, if you so choose, to make some new and possibly healing decisions for your life.

When new information is given to us in this way, we can question with more awareness the assumptions we have made about our past and are making about our present, as well as the mythological models we are using in our lives. From that we can create new truths to help us move forward.*

Although dream incubation was eventually suppressed by the Orthodox Christian Church, it survived in great part within the arcane European shamanic tradition known as the Path of Pollen, in which old accounts record people's amazement at the state of consciousness they arrive at after such incubation, regardless of whether they were awake or asleep or had their eyes open or closed. It is clear from these accounts that they, in fact, entered a state that was neither wakefulness nor sleep, but instead a different reality altogether, a liminal place that might best be described as "betwixt and between."

It is this dreaming practice that is undertaken on Darkness Visible

---

* The technique of working with images in this way (known as *imagework*) was pioneered by the psychoanalyst Dr. Dina Glouberman. Her latest book on the process is *The Joy of Burnout: How the End of the World Can Be a New Beginning* (Makawao, Maui, Hawaii: Inner Ocean Publishing, 2003). The technique is also dealt with at length in *The Journey to You: A Shaman's Path To Empowerment* by Ross Heaven (New York: Bantam, 2001).

retreats. We ask participants to lie down and relax and then use their active imaginations to see, sense, and feel themselves being escorted by beautiful maidens into a healing temple, surrounded by safety and comfort.

Next, they lie down on dreaming cots (sometimes these are hammocks) and are covered with fresh white sheets and aromatic flowers and herbs. Incense burns around them and they drift in visions as they listen to chants, music, and the healing words of priests and physicians. And then Asklepios himself is invoked, and so begins their personal healing journey through their visions.

The scene is set for them using an ancient form of storytelling that is a form of magic rather than entertainment. In this telling, the tale truly comes to life, allowing listeners to step into the landscape of the story. The facilitators move among the participants, spraying the air with perfumes and anointing them with oils and incense. Flower petals are scattered over them and there is chanting, singing, and the sounds of sistrums, gongs, bells, and singing bowls. Prayers are offered to the healing god Asklepios, and then we allow our participants to visit with the priests, priestesses, and gods so they may have their visions and healing may take place.

This is a long process (it usually lasts for many hours); it unfolds and develops deeply and with great power. Participants typically report that a meeting with the gods does indeed come about. They sense the presence of the gods in the room; they see them in the darkness and they feel the healings bestowed on them as they are released from the wounds of the past.

One participant offers this:

> The temple built up around me very quickly and solidly and I could feel the presence of the god and his priestesses moving about us. The use of sounds, [especially] the Tibetan bells, was particularly apt for facilitating this process. On being anointed, I felt myself going deeper and I had several beautiful visitations as I prayed for healing and for the ability to forgive those whom I have perceived to have wronged me. The shadowed form of the god him-

self moved by and blessed me. I was visited by a priestess and we made love . . . an intensely erotic and deeply healing experience.

Marius, another participant, shares this overall assessment:

[It was] truly a magical and mythological time of deep healing and great insights and wonderful meditative rest. After this event [we were] all so much more relaxed and open.

Other participants describe their meeting with the gods with the following words:

Relaxing, calming, and full of wonderment. I was taken to a temple where my body was cleansed and prepared in a sacred way. The music connected with a rhythm in my solar plexus and I felt myself drawn upward.

Everything about me was light. . . . I felt a floating sensation and weightless[ness]. . . . It was as if healing and wisdom had all come together. I did not want to leave.

Completely amazing. [This has] changed my relationship to my dreaming ever since. My general sense of the group was of everyone having a powerful and profound healing experience.

It is important to note that we, as facilitators, do nothing but suggest their encounters. We set and build the invisible landscape and invoke the gods of healing, but it is the participants themselves, through the power of their imagination and dreaming, who open to their interaction with Asklepios and, through him, access their own healing powers.

Our participants are no different from anyone else, and if they can heal themselves, then so can we all. So can you. This ability is a part of our identity that is often underplayed within our world of names and numbers, but we all have this power—in the 95 percent of our brain that our binary society encourages us to leave untapped and unaccessed by our dreaming.

THE POWER OF SILENCE AND THE POWER OF SOUND

The use of silence is a vital component of darkness retreats. Typically, there is a period of twenty-four hours or more in a retreat that is dedicated to a sacred silence.

Conversely, the careful use of words is a skill of shamans the world over, for shamans were the first poets, and their understanding of the power of words is reflected in beliefs around the use of speech.

Bid Ben Bid Bont, a Bee Master from the Path of Pollen, speaks about language and silence in the typically eloquent fashion of the bard:

> Language transmits the thoughts of the speaker, but we cannot grasp the subtle meaning of words unless we drop all precon-
> ceived ideas and listen without referring to our own opinion, which veils comprehension. Thus, silence is often the better me-
> dium for communing.[5]

He goes on to say that at every instant, every thought and gesture modify the invisible weft with which the Fates weave patterns of our destiny—and which we, knowingly or unknowingly, prepare.

The Bee Masters and Mistresses of this lineage, together with other seers of Keltia, well understood that some words could cause harm, even if uttered without ill intent. When wishing good fortune, a person should be as inclusive as possible, for the *gui ghann* (stingy prayer) can cause ill luck to befall those for whom it is made.

The power of the words of Gaelic poets was considered to be enormous, as is illustrated in the belief that both rats and mice obeyed orders given to them in verse. Indeed, if a barn was infested with them, a poet rather than a rat-catcher was called. A further illustration of this is held within the following old Keltic tale:

The ruler of a prosperous kingdom sent for one of his messengers. When he arrived, the king instructed him to go out and find the worst thing in the entire world, and bring it back within days. The messenger departed, and returned a few days later, as instructed. He entered the court empty-handed.

Puzzled, the king asked, "What have you discovered? I see nothing."

The messenger replied, "The worst thing in the world, Your Majesty, is right here," and he stuck out his tongue.

Bewildered, the king asked the young man to explain.

The messenger said, "My tongue, Sire, is the worst thing in the world. My tongue can do many horrible things. It may speak evil and tell lies. I can overindulge with my tongue, which leaves me feeling tired and sick, and I can say things that may wound others. My tongue is the worst thing in the world."

Pleased by what he heard, the king commanded the messenger to go out once more and this time find him the best thing in the world.

The messenger left hurriedly and, once again, came back days later with nothing in his hands.

"Where is it?" the king shouted out.

Again, the messenger stuck out his tongue.

"Tell me," said the king. "How can it be?"

The messenger replied: "My tongue, Sire, is the best thing in the world, for my tongue is a messenger of love. Only with my tongue can I express the overwhelming beauty of poetry. It teaches me refinement in tastes and guides me to choose foods that will nourish my body. My tongue is the best thing in the world because it allows me to chant the names of God."

The king was well satisfied and appointed the messenger foremost among his personal advisors.

This story is in accordance with the teachings of Keltic wise ones in which words and the proper crafting of them are considered extremely important skills, and there is a deep respect for *dea-chaint,* "good speech." The tongue cuts and shapes words as they are passed through the mouth. For this reason, medieval Bee Masters—all of them seers and bards—claimed they had two capsules on their tongues: one full of honey for blessing and praising and the other full of poison for cursing and satire.

This ancient knowing has had new light shone upon it by the work of Dr. Masaru Emoto, who theorizes how water is deeply connected to people's individual and collective consciousness. Drawing from his research Emoto has described the ability of water to absorb, hold, and even retransmit human feelings and emotions. Using high-speed photography, he found that crystals formed in frozen water reveal changes when specific, concentrated thoughts are directed toward them. Music, visual images, words written on paper, and photographs also have an impact on the crystal structure. The conjecture that naturally flows from this—and which is utterly congruant with the shamanic worldview—is that because people are 70 percent water, and Earth is 70 percent water, we can heal our planet and ourselves by consciously expressing positive and prayerful moods and emotions.[6]

Silent darkness also played a key role toward gaining poetic inspiration within the tradition of these Keltic bards. Such silence involved a ritual of lying in the dark to undertake composition, a practice recorded up to the time of the "last of the bards," Fearflatha O Gnimh, who lived in the seventeenth century.

This application of silence and darkness is explored in Darkness Visible retreats in the form of a daily writing discipline undertaken as the first task of every new day, when the state of being "betwixt and between" is heightened and when liminal zones, as the poets muse, can be best accessed.

The methods we use in our retreats draw upon the Keltic tradition in which great emphasis is placed upon "secret" veins of poetry within a person's body—the *feithna filiochta*. The primary vein is seen as being situated at the back of the head, moving into and arriving at the area of the pineal gland. It is known as the "hidden eye of genius" or the "strong eye of the shaman"—that which allows the seer to witness visible darkness.

Gaelic poets knew that, when one lay down and composed in darkness, the back of the head was an unseen or "dark" part of the body. It was thought that, when the poet began to compose, the blood began to pulsate through his veins and the meter of the poem corresponded to the rhythm of this pulsation. These veins are part of a Keltic system of seership akin to the meridian maps that are now better known from the Chinese system of acupuncture. Another of these secret veins, believed to run from the heart to the third finger of the left hand, is said to be the reason why it is customary to wear a wedding ring on that finger. The longest finger on the right hand is said to have a conduit to the life center; Keltic folklore tells us that a drop of blood taken from this vein can cure many forms of skin ailments.

In darkness, many of us can perceive the maps and channels of energy within the body. This perception not only affords us new ways of sensing the flow of energies that dictate well-being, but is a means of experiencing the world more holistically. For example, during one Darkness Visible exercise where we play temple bells, gongs, and chants to our participants, people often remark that the sounds are heard not by the ears but by the energy centers of the body. Kathy, on a 2005 retreat, commented that the bells sounded "like stars exploding in my heart, their energy reverberating around my body. I didn't exactly *hear* the sound, not with my ears at least, I sort of *felt* it with my being."

This is somewhat consistent with recent psychological findings, which show that the emotional centers react to sound before the brain interprets or even formally registers the content of that sound as communication. The results demonstrate, among other things, that "*how* a person says something often transmits more emotional information than *what* he says."[7] Tone of voice and quality of sound are therefore important and convey emotional information that colors the entire communication before it is even deciphered.

The power of words is even more profoundly felt during the day of silence on our retreats. Participants subsequently remark that the words and tone used by the facilitators to direct and guide them on that day are experienced at a deep emotional level and they speak of being "extremely open" and "vulnerable" at this time so that "words of love, tenderness, and gentle guidance" are experienced as a warmth throughout the body and carry far more weight than would normally be the case.

In part this may also tie in with other findings from the psychology of creativity, which have shown that "the more [we lose our] social and language abilities, the wilder and freer [our] art [becomes]."[8] While in silence, participants are much closer to their emotions and their creative selves and so make connections at a deeper level and hear with more intensity, so that even nuances of tone seem vast and meaningful. We might change the quotation above, in fact, to say that the more we lose our social and language abilities, the more we actually *listen* to the world and hear with our entire bodies and souls, the wilder and freer our *hearts* become.

TRY THIS

⬤ What's Your Name?

Shamans commonly observe that no matter what our given names, we all have a spirit name we have carried with us from the time before we were born, and that this name both connects us to the power of the universe and offers us clues to what we came here to do.

Close your eyes and see yourself back in the cave you visited during the exercise "The Cave of Souls" (page 35). One of the tunnels in the cave takes you deeper into the earth and, eventually, out of the cave and into the dim light of another world, a place of primal and harmonious forces that exists beneath the world we know.

When you enter this place, you will find yourself on a path that takes you into a deep forest and further into darkness. Here, before a mighty and ancient tree, the path you have been following comes to an end.

At this tree you find someone waiting for you—a beautiful spirit woman or man who recognizes you and is pleased to see you there. This being leans toward you and whispers your spirit name. Breathe it in and thank him or her for this information, then turn around and retrace your steps back to this earthly reality at this moment in time.

Open your eyes and write down your spirit name. What does it look like? How does it sound? What sort of charge do you get from it? What does it mean to you?

Conduct a bit of research into your name (if it's an animal name, for example, find out the characteristics and qualities of the animal it represents) and see what clues it might hold to the work you came here to do and the experience of your life so far, as well as to the future(s) you could choose for yourself.

⬤ The Ancestral Chain

Once you have completed the exercise "Ancestor Visualization" (pages 121–23) and healed the first wounding event in your ancestral history, close your eyes again and let yourself dream across the generations, noticing how that family curse has been in some way carried forward. It can end with you, if you wish, so it does not have to be passed on.

A specific ritual can be performed to accomplish this. First, find a straight stick and then hold it to your stomach, the place in the body where our early memories are stored. Feel all the energy that is not serving you pouring out of your body and into the stick.

When you are satisfied that there is none of this energy left inside of you, break the stick into as many pieces as you wish, choosing the emotion you want to invest in this action, then take the pieces outside and bury them.

Believe, without a doubt, that this issue is now dead and gone.

◖ Temple Dreaming

> *Perhaps your dream drifted from mine*
> *And through the dark sea was seeking me*
> *While the dark Earth spins*
> *Neither night nor sleep could separate us*
>
> PABLO NERUDA, "NIGHT ON THE ISLAND"

Plan a night of opulence for yourself: Scatter some rugs and comfortable pillows around, spray the air with perfume, fill the room with flowers, take a relaxing bath, play some soothing music (music without lyrics is best). Then lie down in the temple you have created for yourself and close your eyes. Breathe deeply and evenly into the space between the heart and solar plexus, the part of the body that the ancients saw as the place of the soul.

Ask and intend that the healing gods will come to you and that you will receive the blessings that you need. Be aware of your images during this time. In Asklepian temple dreaming, it was believed that the healing of the soul took place through the images themselves.

You are welcome, if you wish, to simply fall asleep and dream!

◖ A Blessing for Yourself

Poetry comes from the quiet mind and from behind closed eyes. In the Keltic bardic tradition, poets were the carriers of blessings and inspiration from the gods. A poet, it is said, would lie down beside a river in a dark forest, holding a rock upon his belly, in that place of the soul, so that his spirit would not fly away and he could take his dreaming inward.

Close your eyes and lie down in the same way, offering a prayer to the gods and muses of verse that the words of a blessing be given to you in a poem that will be yours.

The following blessing for protection and grace comes from an old Keltic script:

The love and affection of the angels be to you,
The love and affection of the saints be to you,
The love and affection of heaven be to you,
To guard and to cherish you.

May God shield you on every steep,
May Christ aid you on every path,
May Spirit fill you on every slope,
On hill and on plain.[9]

Now see what words your own inspiration brings you.

8

Welcome Home
Coming out of Darkness into Darkness

Now I pierce the darkness—new beings appear.
The earth recedes from me into the night.

WALT WHITMAN, "THE SLEEPERS," *LEAVES OF GRASS*

THE EXISTENTIAL PSYCHOANALYST Viktor Frankl wrote of our "will to meaning," which he defined as "the basic striving of man to find a meaning and purpose" in life. This meaning comes most easily from our engagement with the world and with others and from a sense that there is something bigger than ourselves, some mystery or magic of which we are a part, "something or someone other than oneself . . . a cause to serve or a person to love."[1]

This self-transcendence is essential for our health and happiness, because it allows us to forget, rather than forsake, ourselves—that is, to overcome our sense of separateness, aloneness, and distance from God. "Only to the extent to which man fulfills a meaning out there in the world, does he fulfill himself."[2]

In a culture such as ours, it is not surprising that so many of us are searching for meaning: values are focused on the individual; we have seen a breakdown in our communities and traditional ways of relating to others;

140

and we have witnessed the loss of the extended family (indeed, the loss of the family itself, given that most marriages now end in divorce). Far from feeling that we belong to something greater than ourselves, we do not even fully know who we are. This is the fallout from the Fall: in our separation from God, we have built a world in this image—one of division and isolation in which we are alone and removed from our source.

According to Frankl, this produces an "existential vacuum," a sense of meaninglessness or emptiness and a boredom with life evidenced by that listless feeling that many of us experience when we are not fully immersed in or distracted by our lives; when we realize that there is nowhere to go and no one to be . . . except ourselves.

This feeling is widespread in the twenty-first century as a result of our industrialization, dehumanization, and lack of connection with others. Indeed, Frankl believed this aimlessness was the main reason people came to him for therapy. They felt that their lives had no purpose, challenge, or adventure, and when they tried to fill this emptiness with work, power, money, sex, or material things, it merely reinforced the shallowness of their lives until, craving a sense of something more than this artificiality, they collapsed into mental unease. "The feeling of meaninglessness not only underlies the mass neurotic triad of today, i.e., depression-addiction-aggression, but also may eventuate in . . . neurosis."[3]

What we are essentially talking about here, once again, is our need for a ritual modern society most lacks: initiation into a world beyond the isolated frontiers of the self alone, into a meaning for existence that is bigger than the trivial ambitions of fame, fortune, and celebrity that have been handed to us as a manifesto and an empty panacea for our problems, "if only to prevent our souls from falling asleep."[4]

Immersion in darkness serves as this initiation for many participants in Darkness Visible—but there is always an end to every initiation, a time when the boy or girl must return home to the village as a man or woman. For our participants this comes with the ceremony of unveiling, when the Mindfold is removed and they see the world again, this time with eyes washed clean by the dark.

Before we look at some participants' reactions to this new world and how it felt to have their sight restored, it is instructive to consider the experience of others who have emerged from an even deeper darkness.

PASSAGE FROM DARKNESS: A RECOVERY FROM BLINDNESS

Historically, there has been almost no hope of recovery from long-term blindness. Of the more than one million blind people in America today and the more than two million who are anticipated to lose their vision as the baby boom generation ages, most will remain without sight.

Now, however, largely due to the work of Dr. William Dobelle, there is a real possibility that the blind may be able to see again.* Dobelle has been working on an artificial eye since 1968, based on research showing that electrical stimulation of the brain's visual cortex enables blind people to see small points of light, called phosphenes. By teaching patients to "connect the dots" of these points of light, a level of effective vision can be restored.

The Dobelle implant is actually a three-part system comprising a miniature video camera mounted on a pair of eyeglasses, which the patient wears; a computer processor that translates video images into signals the brain can understand; and an implant that electrically stimulates the visual cortex of the brain. Once this system is operational, patients can see, although the images themselves do not exactly equate to normal vision. Objects appear in a dot matrix pattern. The next step, then, is teaching people how to interpret these images that reach their brain, for those who have never been sighted will have only felt objects before and must learn how to translate the feel of an object into its visual appearance.

In 1978 a man named Jerry received the first Dobelle implant. At first he could see only shades of gray in a limited field of vision, but his sight gradually improved until he was able to navigate the subway on his own and perform other feats that the sighted take for granted, but

---

*See, for example, www.cbc.ca/sunday/sight/procedure.html and http://news.bbc.co.uk/2/hi/science/nature/606938.stm.

that were previously difficult or impossible for him to accomplish.

More recently, Jens Naumann received a second-generation Dobelle implant. Tests show that he can now navigate quite easily, find things in an apartment, and even drive a car around a parking lot. As a result of this success, Dobelle predicts that by the end of this century, Braille and guide dogs will be part of the past.

What the research does not tell us, however, is how newly sighted people feel about or experience their "new" world now that they can engage with it more fully. What does our world mean to someone who sees it for the first time? As we noted earlier in this book, Kogi priests-to-be spend nineteen years in darkness, and when they emerge from their shadowed caves to actually see the world, their souls fill with awe at its beauty. Some of the people that scientists like Dobelle have helped may have been blind for longer than nineteen years. In fact—unlike the Kogi—some have never been sighted, not even in infancy or early childhood. What do they make of the world as they step out of darkness?

Current research that tells of the existential and metaphysical sensations of these people is simply not available. But we can look back more than forty years to the work of Richard Gregory and Jean Wallace with a patient they called SB.[5] If these results are in any way typical of what it is like to regain sight after a prolonged time in darkness (as it seems they are), then they are not at all what we might expect.

INTO THE LIGHT

SB was effectively blind from birth, and it was not until the age of fifty-two, when he underwent two corneal grafting operations, that he finally recovered his sight. This fascinated Gregory and Wallace, who were particularly interested in finding an answer to the question first posed by Molyneux to the philosopher John Locke (1632–1704):

> Suppose a man born blind, and now adult, and taught by his touch
> to distinguish between a cube and a sphere of the same metal.

Suppose then the cube and the sphere were placed on a table and the blind man made to see. . . . Could he distinguish and tell which was the globe and which the cube?[6]

What Gregory and Wallace found was, with a few exceptions, much as Locke himself concluded: years spent in darkness, "seeing" only with the hands, meant that the blind person whose vision was restored needed to learn to see all over again, this time with the eyes.

In the case of SB, there were a few objects he could identify without using touch, but he usually guessed at these by essentially tracing their outlines with his eyes, much as he used his hands. What he saw that really filled him with joy and surprise, however, were those things that he could never have touched. When he first saw the crescent moon three days after his sight-restoring operation, he expressed amazement, expecting it to look like a slice of cake; and he became fascinated by mirrors and reflections, which, of course, contain their information at a depth beneath the surface of the glass, unavailable to touch.

What shocked the researchers, however (although they didn't fully explore this), was SB's emotional reaction to his new world of sight. Gregory and Wallace likely anticipated what we all might: a sense of joy and liberation from a man who could now see after fifty-two years of darkness. Immediately after his operation, however, SB began to comment on the drabness of the world. "The one spontaneous comment [of excitement and happiness that] SB made to us [one] evening was to describe the colors in the sky at sunset." Then the sunset vanished: "[W]e came down a hill and it all disappeared. . . . He seemed dispirited, and indeed he never seemed the cheerful rather extravert [blind] man he was at the hospital when we first saw him."

SB found modern life disappointing and intimidating: "He found the traffic frightening and would not attempt to cross even a comparatively small street by himself. This was in marked contrast to his former behavior, as described to us by his wife, when he would cross any street in his own town by himself. . . . He seemed to lack confidence and interest in his surroundings."

Six months later, the situation was no better: "We formed a strong impression that his sight was to him almost entirely disappointing [and that] he had lost more than he had gained by [its] recovery."

SB died in August 1960, about seven years after undergoing the operation, his feelings never really having lifted. Gregory and Wallace concluded that "his story is in some ways tragic. He suffered one of the greatest handicaps and yet he lived with energy and enthusiasm. When his handicap was apparently swept away, as by a miracle, he lost his peace and his self-respect. We may feel disappointment at a private dream come true: SB found disappointment with what he took to be reality."

Though it may seem curious to us, SB's response to his personal "miracle" is not so unusual. In the early 1800s, Franz Anton Mesmer wrote of a patient whose eyesight returned but, rather than joy, she experienced only sadness and confusion as a consequence:

> How is it that I now find myself less happy than before? Everything that I see causes me disagreeable emotions. Oh, I was much more at ease in my blindness. . . . If I were always to feel such uneasiness as I do at present at the sight of new things, I would rather sooner return on the spot to my former blindness.[7]

Another early psychologist, Beer, also noticed the uneasiness of patients whose sight was returned to them:

> Among the most remarkable psychological phenomena presented to my observation in all the patients so far operated upon, is the rapid and complete loss of that striking and wonderful serenity which is characteristic only of those who have never yet seen; for hardly are the first lively sallies of their curiosity satisfied after the operation, than already they evince this striking transformation of their attitude. Gloomy and reserved, they now shun for a time the society of others. . . .[8]

Why would newly sighted individuals respond in this way when they gain a sense through which they can fully absorb the wonder of the world—a sense that inspires awe in the Kogi priest who emerges from his own dark cave? Sadly, the answer seems to be that the modern world is just not that wonderful. It is telling, for example, that the two occasions when SB truly experienced awe and excitement at his world were in relation to nature: the beauty of a sunset and the fascination of the crescent moon. These are sights that have always moved us and connected with our souls. By contrast, Gregory and Wallace tell us that "he [SB] seemed changed when he came to London; dispirited and bored."

We imagine, in our arrogance and ignorance, that it is the man-made glory of the conquered world that should inspire and amaze those who can see and share in its splendor, but in fact it is the natural world that sings to us, just as it does to the Kogi priest. When SB was forced to endure trips to London, the Science Museum (a monument to man's ingenuity in the control of natural forces) and the zoo (man's ability to tame and cage nature), he merely became depressed.

A letter to the researchers by SB's wife seems to confirm this. Commenting on her husband's emotional state, she writes, in melancholy words: "It seems to me our world is not grand as we thought and [my husband] did not know the way people acted—until he got his sight."

In addition, as a person without sight, SB was considered to be very independent and extremely able. When he regained his sight and found a job, however, he was regarded as somewhat backward and incapable because of skills (such as reading and writing) that he had never been able to gain. He was ridiculed and teased by his workmates and eventually suffered a stress-related illness. When this caused him to take time off from work, the only offer of help he received was for psychiatric care.

What this suggests specifically is that we lack understanding of the gifts of darkness and what the newly sighted might be able to teach us; and broadly, that our society lacks respect, care, and true community. When the Kogi priest emerges from his cave, by contrast, he is welcomed by the community and revered as a great spiritual teacher.

What we are talking about is the breakdown of connection and compassion in our fragmented society, due, in no small part, to the lack of an initiatory procedure that can teach us how to relate as human beings to all the members of our society and to respect the part each of us plays for the good of all.

THE COMMITMENT AT THE CROSSROADS

In many tribal societies, the place where roads cross is regarded as holy ground. The cross itself, even in Christianized countries, is a symbol of power that represents the meeting of spirit (the vertical arm) and matter (the horizontal arm).

In the design of the Keltic cross there is also a circle that connects and surrounds the point where these two planes meet. It represents unity, symbolizes the rejoining of God and man, and respects the sacred nature of both the material and immaterial worlds. In Haiti, money is often left at crossroads because the Loa Baron is one of the spirits there, and the spirits must always be paid for their help—in this case, for safe passage. Baron also represents the coming together of spirit and matter and the paradox of opposites in union. He is the father of the dead and caretaker of the cemetery, but also the protector of new life in the form of children. Despite his role in the land of the dead, he is also a great healer for the living and is petitioned when all other spiritual appeals have failed, for no one can die if Baron has refused to dig their grave.

The crossroads, then, is a place of power and potential. From its center, we can take many paths, representing our many opportunities and possible directions in life. Thus, before they are returned to sight, Darkness Visible participants are led to a crossroads and stand at its center. They are told where they are and the symbolism of the place in which they stand, and they are then offered three choices: (1) They can take one step backward, physically and metaphorically, into the life they knew and the world they were a part of before they were taken by the darkness. (2) They can remain where they are and, even when the retreat is over, continue to consider their options and make their commitment at a later date. (3) Or they can take a step forward, representing a promise to bring back into their sighted life all they have learned from darkness and thereby live in a new and more fulfilling way.

Just as SB learned, the choice is not as easy as it seems to be. As one participant wrote: "I know I want to grow, but there was something that morning that really had me doubting what I was committing to. . . . This may sound strange, and I was baffled myself."

Such reticence is understandable. This is a real commitment, an opportunity for change and a chance to leave the past behind. Such commitments are not empty words; they demand action—sometimes life-changing action—in the "real world" if we are to live in integrity and not disappoint ourselves. Another initiate offered: "This was for me not just an act or a promise; it was a duty—a duty to myself. I was happy to share it [with the others, and] to know that all had taken their steps and made their choices. I know that the step I took was a great one in the direction of 'me.' "

This appointment at the crossroads goes far beyond notions of duty for some participants. For some, it is an opportunity to completely shed the skin of their old lives.

> The commitment at the crossroads was like being reborn and felt like a chance to leave the past behind. I see the light of love up ahead drawing me forward. My tears flowed as I let my total vulnerability show.
>
> I choose to go forward rather than stay where I am. This is a hard path to travel but one I know I must take by making a commitment to myself and letting my vulnerability show.

Kevin, the participant who shares his accounts extensively in chapter 3, offers this of his crossroads experience:

> It felt very fitting and very empowering to once again formally and in community stand before my ancestors and dedicate myself

to them. When I took that step forward I felt like a Keltic warrior ready for battle; a fiery man of dreams and poems.

I saw a form coalescing from the brilliant sunlight. (Although I was still wearing the Mindfold, it felt dazzlingly bright on the other side of it; I could feel the sun beating on the outside.) Much to my surprise, two long, graceful antlers began to form, and then before me was a stag of light. It was Herne/Pan, not quite as I'd ever seen him before, [but] composed of dancing, humming sparks of sunlight. I sent him greetings and he acknowledged my renewed commitment. Then he dissolved into spinning fragments of light, becoming part of the photons that bombarded me, seeking entrance.

THE UNVEILING: RETURNING TO THE SIGHTED WORLD

Finally, after they have made their choice at the crossroads, the time comes for these voyagers into darkness to return to the land of sight. Do they experience this return in the same way that SB and the patients of Beer and Mesmer did, who were so disappointed at the reality of the world?

As the time came to take off the blindfold, I did not want to do it as I didn't feel ready. The darkness had become my friend and I still wanted to cling to its walls. The process of emerging from the dark was scary. I was crying, feeling totally vulnerable, my heart wide open.

This was not as I anticipated at all. I seemed to slip back into a world of seeing without any great emotion. I appreciated the beauty of the natural world but, if anything, this was somehow dimmed in comparison to my previous multisensorial appreciation in the darkness and brought me back into a more "mental" space. Having said that, seeing the faces of my fellow voyagers and feeling the hushed awe of the moment of return was something that shall remain with me always as a vision of beauty and import.

This was very painful for me. My eyes did not want to see the light, my heart was opened up and fragile, and I knew that the world would not understand and give me space. I was afraid to face the light of day again. But when I could see nature was more beautiful than ever, more alive and more special, it was like seeing with new eyes, perceiving with new senses. I remember just smiling so much at everything and everyone. It was truly an amazing time. I know others felt like I did as well, but somehow, with darkness gone, the connection to the others seemed not so strong.

I was surprised that the feelings I had after about twenty minutes were rather normal (not that I consider the world normal . . . it was just my "normal").

The answer—perhaps sadly—is that just as it was for SB, there is a sense that the world we have created, and to which our participants know they must return, holds no fascination for them. There is instead a feeling on the part of some that they would prefer to remain in the dark world, where at least they felt connected to others and more in touch with themselves.

Also, just as for SB, a vision of the natural world and a sense of expanded communion with nature, rather than man-made reality, was what most moved some participants. Cedric wrote, "I felt a greater affinity with nature; I actually felt a part of it." And Kevin commented:

The light that fell upon my eyes felt more sacred to me than before. . . . The world had become ensouled.

The land spread before me, peaceful, utterly beautiful and complete within itself. The emotion I felt was love. . . . Trees, plants, sky, sun, clouds . . . were all dancing [and] the tune they dance to, I realized, is love.

I sat there for a long time, savoring this sweetness, this almost unbearable intensity. I became aware of trees, the soft, rich grass, and a yellow flower held me entranced. After a time, I was aware of coming more into ordinary consciousness, but this wasn't a concern because I felt I could tune in to [this other] consciousness at will.

Louise had a similar experience:

As I am led outdoors onto a soft grassy carpet, I can feel the warmth of the sun on my face. I lift my face to the sun and surrender myself totally, as I realize I need the light and the sun in order to grow and move forward.

There is a blanket over my head and sunglasses to shield my eyes. I remove the blindfold with my eyes shut tight and my hands over my eyes under the blanket. As I remove the blanket with my eyes still shut tight I see God—a brilliant ball of red, orange, swirling, growing, honeycombed energy. It is the most amazing force of all.

I see that God is in everything and believe that I have truly seen God in all of life. Everything is bright, clear, sharp and full of energy. Colors, shapes, are all there in minute detail. I am seeing with new eyes. I feel newborn, calm and at peace, with a sense of wonderment at this world around me.

Sadly, rather than being positively affected by the world of the light, it seems we are most affected by time spent in darkness, exploring the majesty of the soul and, ironically, the deeper connection we have to others in a world without sight and judgment. On their return to a sighted world, it is only nature that sustains those who have spent time in darkness; it is nature that allows them to "tune in to [this other] consciousness" again.

We recall again the words of Milton in *Paradise Lost*, that these great "flames" of the modern world—"progress," the city, "civilization"—do not bring us light, "but rather darkness visible"; and those of Marianne Williamson as quoted by Nelson Mandela, that "it is our light, not our darkness, that most frightens us."

How can we change our world so that people are not "afraid to face the light of day again"? The solution is blindingly obvious—but far from easy. We need to re-enchant our world, to call back its soul and allow its spirit to flourish. On a practical level this demands a radical reassessment of our lives and goals at the most fundamental political, social, and economic levels. It means the active rebirthing of communities that can nourish us; a political and social system based on new ideals instead of conflict and division; an economic ideology that does not regard individuals as commodities and greater materialism as the solution to every problem; and an education system that, rather than causing us to lose 95 percent of ourselves, encourages us to dream our dreams. It calls for our return to a respect for others and a respect for ourselves. And, decidedly, it calls for a process of initiation—not into a system, but into life itself, into our natural being, so that we can find the meaning that we need.

> *Nature, whose sweet rains fall on just and unjust alike, will have clefts in the rocks where I may hide, and secret valleys in whose silence I may weep undetected. She will hang the night with stars so that I may walk abroad in the darkness without stumbling, and send the wind over my footprints so that none may track me to my hurt: she will cleanse me in great waters, and with bitter herbs make me whole.*
>
> OSCAR WILDE, *DE PROFUNDIS*

TRY THIS
The Meaning of Life

Imagine you have a magical craft: a time machine. Climb aboard and set the controls so it takes you forward to the moment just before your death.

In that moment, you realize with regret that there have been a number of things you haven't said or done when you had the chance. You always meant to, but you simply ran out of time or other concerns became more pressing . . . and now it is too late. What are the things you haven't done, the opportunities you most regret having missed?

Now return yourself in your craft to the present, with the conviction that you will do and say the things you wished you had at the imagined moment of your death. Then travel forward again, to the moment before your death, this time aware that you have no regrets; you've said and done all that you wanted to. How do you feel now? What in your life has made you happiest and most fulfilled?

Return to the present in your time machine.

We are happiest doing and saying what gives us meaning. What we haven't done—but wish we had—provides clues to who we really are, to who and what we love, to where our passion lies.

Without question, you have the choice to live a life of meaning or one that brings regret.

The Sadness of the World

We have created a strange world of sadness for ourselves, a place in which blind people given the gift of sight would rather return to their darkness.

There is a Buddhist practice to help us deal with the sorrow of the world and the sorrows we hold within us. Called *tonglen,* it seeks to help us release old fears and open our hearts so that we can be truly present and filled with compassion (which, incidentally, means "shared sorrow").

Close your eyes and bring to mind any suffering you have. Perhaps it is the pain of a broken home or a lost love. Breathe into that pain. As you inhale, see all your attachments to it being drawn into your body, like strands of light. Let them enter you with form and fill you completely so that you can sense their color, shape, size, temperature, texture, and mood and can taste and smell and hear them.

Then expand your compassion, breathing in the suffering of every child abandoned or lover betrayed, until you feel the sorrows of the whole world on your soul.

Now breathe out compassion—for yourself and for all those who suffer as you do. You know the pain of others, and the light of love radiates from you, bright and gold and vast, from your heart to theirs.

As you breathe in and out, you transmute the energy of this pain, turning pain into love and tears into kindness toward all the sentient beings who need our support and understanding in this sad and beautiful world.

◐ The Crossroads Commitment

We all stand at a crossroads, no matter where we are in our lives. There are infinite paths we could walk and many choices to make. Every decision, every second of the day, will alter our course in some way and take us in a different direction, but it is commitment—to one course of action, one way of being, and one road to travel—that will take us where we really want to go.

Now that you have worked through the exercises in this book (especially "The Voices Within," page 76; "The Conception Journey," pages 94–97; "Who Are You?," page 112; and "The Meaning of Life," page 152), you also have a decision to make. You can return to who you thought you were or who you used to be; you can stay where you are; or you can apply these lessons and become someone new. But you can't forego making a decision; even a decision not to decide is a decision in itself.

Close your eyes and see yourself standing at the center of a crossroads. One arrow points to Old Me, one to New Me, and one to Just Stay Here. Explore each option. Walk a little way along each path, see who you meet there and how it looks to you. Then, when you are ready, come back to the center.

Now it is time for commitment. Breathe in and take a step in any of these directions.

Which did you choose? And why?

Beginning to See the Light
Life after Darkness

I was in the darkness; I could not see my words nor the
wishes of my heart.
Then suddenly there was a great light—
Let me into the darkness again.

STEPHEN CRANE, "I WAS IN THE DARKNESS"

One does not become enlightened by imagining figures of light,
but by making the darkness conscious.

C. G. JUNG, *ALCHEMICAL STUDIES*

LOOKING BACK ON the time that our retreat participants spent in the dark caves of their souls, how can we define the meaning of their experience—spiritually, emotionally, mentally, and in a practical sense? What, if anything, do they now do differently? What changes have they made to their lives, following their commitment at the crossroads?

Commonly, upon reemerging into the light and reintegrating into "normal" life, our participants' spirits widen. The dark is no longer a place to fear. When we emerge from darkness and feel the sunlight warm our eyes and see people walking, playing, going about their business, we may look at them more compassionately, more intensely, because in darkness we have learned to see them without judgment.

For perhaps extended periods of time, we still see purely and let the world speak to us in a language deeper than words, a language from the seabed of humanity, where the gods used to whisper to us about our essential nature. A gentle soaring ebb and flow holds us for a while during our transition from the dark realms to the communality of eyes, from a private world to a shared world, from solitude to sun.

When the former Beirut hostage Brian Keenan was released after four and a half years in captivity, much of that time spent in darkness, he marveled at what he saw around him and, for a time at least, was able to regard the world in a different way. "I emerged from what was a very heightened reality to somewhere quite else. I would study the intricate patterns of moss growing on granite, I would view the trees that had been shaped by the winds. I was clear that I was being drawn into things and seeing things that I would not normally have seen."[1]

This profound impact of reencountering light and returning to the world once more is mirrored in the experience of those who emerge from the darkness retreat.

> In that sacred time and space I experienced a glimpse of what love may really be about and how it may also be possible for me to have it in my life. This was the beginning of an incredible journey for me, which continues in even greater intensity to this day.
>
> On a physical and practical sense, I moved from London to Penzance [a more rural community in England] as a direct result of the work. I felt deeply held in the arms of this magical land and [had] a sense of homecoming. It seemed to me the darkness allowed a clarity—removed from the mental and connected to the heart and spirit—that [enabled] that which could have remained as a wishful ideal to become manifest. . . . I have experienced a profound and sacred communion in my life.

Another participant said she felt the darkness experience to be "a validation of my faith in myself. . . . It was awe-inspiring to see beneath the visual surface of things, to see energy in its primal state, and to then communicate with the archetypal forms it takes. I am left with the realization that 'All you need is love.'"

For others, the impact has been far more practical than emotional but, perhaps, even more life-affirming in terms of its implications: "I am prepared to put more effort into doing a better job than was [previously] the case. The rush to finish no longer seems as important."

Darkness sparks within us a realization of who we are, the potential we contain beyond and beneath the material world, and the seed of opportunity we all have within ourselves to be who we always knew we could be.

Perhaps the last word should go to one participant, Lisa, whose account in many ways sums up the darkness experience, as well as our human condition, as the greatest paradox of all: we are spiritual and physical beings who know so little of the vast unknown within us and who struggle to come to terms with this divided world in which we seem always to be battling for a sense of our true selves and to find our way back to God.

> After the event, I felt refreshed and totally alive [and] I had a deep sense of well-being for many months. I made a commitment to myself to live more fully and to see the world with different eyes. . . . I became a little more centered. . . . I talked to people more openly and shared my new sense of well-being with a chosen few.
>
> Then I sort of drifted for a long time and it felt like I lost the connection I had when I was with the group. It was also a time of settling into my state and not really doing very much of anything other than work and day-to-day stuff. This was in contrast to how I felt immediately after the event. I think I could have made more effort to stay in touch [with] and connect to people in the group, as I had feelings of isolation and loneliness and nobody with whom to share the experiences.

I don't know that I have made any major changes in my life other than being more aware of and open to people and experiences. But the feeling of peace of the whole darkness experience has stayed with me and I can recall it and tap into it at any time.

My overall assessment of what this experience meant for me is in the openness of my words here. My willingness to see inside myself and be vulnerable. It was a truly amazing and wonderful experience, which I hope is going to stay with me and continue to grow and [to] guide me on my spiritual path.

I have amazed myself at the way I have allowed myself to be touched and opened up by this experience, as I am most definitely not your average . . . "spiritual" person.

I really have found a new depth within myself and am surprised to find myself reaching for more new depths and dimensions.

The shaman, he who "sees in the dark," might postulate that there is ultimately no such thing as darkness, but merely the inability to truly see. Darkness itself is healing, and the experience of entering it allows us a new possibility to reinvent and reexperience ourselves, though the work of our lives in light will never be easy again.

It is to the credit and the honor of the modern-day pioneers into darkness quoted throughout this book that they were courageous enough to experience this initiation into themselves and the exploration of their fruitful, dark inner spaces. And it is thanks to the ancestors, the elders, and the wisdom-keepers who blazed the trail into darkness in very different times that this pathway has been illuminated for those who have followed in their wake.

We sense there is some sort of spirit that loves birds and the animals
and the ants
Perhaps the same one who gave a radiance to you in your mother's
womb
Is it logical you would be walking around entirely orphaned now?
The truth is you turned away yourself and decided to go into the dark
alone

KABIR

Notes

PREFACE

1. Fragment from Linda Gregg's poem "Different Not Less," *Too Bright to See & Alma* (Saint Paul, Minn.: Graywolf Press, 2002).

CHAPTER 1

1. Bhagwan Shree Rajneesh, *Theologia Mystica: Discourses on the Treatise of St. Dionysius* (Pune, India: Rajneesh Foundation International, 1983).
2. Diane K. Osborn, ed., *Reflections on the Art of Living: A Joseph Campbell Companion* (New York: HarperPerennial, 1991).
3. Paul Devereux, "Speaking in Tongues: The Moody Interview," *Fortean Times* 197, (2005).
4. Malidoma Patrice Somé, *Of Water and the Spirit: Ritual, Magic, and Initiation in the Life of an African Shaman* (New York: Penguin, Arkana Books, 1995).
5. Tenzin Wangyal Rinpoche, *Wonders of the Natural Mind* (Ithaca, N.Y.: Snow Lion Publications, 2000).
6. Ibid.
7. Reuters Wire Service, "Scientists Battle 'Dark Energy' Theory of Universe," March 22, 2005. Story at: http://story.news.yahoo.com.
8. Ibid.
9. Ibid.

CHAPTER 2

1. Johnny Cash in *Mojo* magazine (November 2004).
2. Ibid.
3. Ibid.
4. Ibid.
5. Ken Moritsugu, Knight Ridder, "All Members of Primitive Tribe Survived Tsunami," *Yahoo! News*, 3 March 2005.
6. Brian Keenan, *An Evil Cradling: The Five-Year Ordeal of a Hostage* (London: Random House, 1992).
7. Wade Davis, *One River* (New York: Simon and Schuster, 1997).
8. Julian of Norwich, *Showings* (Mahwah, N.J.: Paulist Press, 1977).
9. Ibid.
10. Emile Male and Dora Nussey, *The Gothic Image: Religious Art in France of the Thirteenth Century* (New York: HarperCollins, 1973).
11. Ibid.

CHAPTER 3

1. Wade Davis, *One River*.
2. Ibid.
3. Ibid.

CHAPTER 4

1. *Angels in the Mirror: Vodou Music of Haiti* (Roslyn, N.Y.: Ellipsis Arts, 1997).
2. Marianne Szegedy-Maszak, "Your Unconscious Makes 95% of Your Decisions," US News.com, reprinted at www.mindpowernews.com/Unconscious.htm.
3. Ibid.
4. M. DelMonte, "Constructivist View of Meditation," *American Journal of Psychotherapy* 41, no. 2 (1987): 286–98.
5. Marion Sonnenmoser, "Friend or Foe?" *Scientific American Mind* 16, no. 1 (2005).
6. Steve J. Ayan, "Right Brain May Be Wrong," *Scientific American Mind* 16, no. 1 (2005).
7. John Sturgeon, *The Psychology of Isolation*, www.space.edu/LibraryResearch/undgrant.html.

8. Donald O. Hebb, *The Organization of Behavior* (Hoboken, N.J.: John Wiley and Sons, 1949).

9. Ibid.

10. I. Altman and W. W. Haythorn, "The Ecology of Isolated Groups," *Behavioral Science* 12 (1967): 169–82, and I. Altman and W. W. Haythorn, "The Effects of Social Isolation and Group Composition on Performance," *Human Relations* 20 (1967): 313–39.

11. John Lilly, *The Centre of the Cyclone* (London: Marion Boyars, 2001).

12. Michael Hutchinson, *The Book of Floating: Exploring the Private Sea* (Nevada City, Calif.: Gateways Books and Tapes, 2003).

13. In Ross Heaven, *The Journey to You: A Shaman's Path to Empowerment* (New York: Bantam, 2001).

14. Ibid.

15. Ibid.

16. Ibid.

17. Ibid.

18. Untitled news story, *Psychology Today*, July/August 1995.

CHAPTER 5

1. Apuleius, *The Golden Ass*, E. J. Kenny, Trans., Penguin Classics new ed. (New York: Penguin Books, 1999).

2. Robert Moore and Douglas Gillette, *King, Warrior, Magician, Lover: Rediscovering the Archetypes of the Mature Masculine* (San Francisco: HarperSanFrancisco, 1999).

CHAPTER 6

1. Don J. Snyder, *Of Time and Memory: My Parents' Love Story* (New York: Ballantine, 2001).

2. A. Pascual-Leone and F. Torres, "Plasticity of the Sensorimotor Cortex Representation of the Reading Finger in Braille Readers," Bethesda, Md.: Human Cortical Physiology Unit, National Institute of Neurological Disorders and Stroke, National Institutes of Health.

3. H. Theoret, L. Merabet, A. Pascual-Leone, "Behavioral and Neuroplastic Changes in the Blind: Evidence for Functionally Relevant Cross-Modal Interactions," Laboratory for Magnetic Brain Stimulation, Department

of Neurology, Beth Israel Deaconess Medical Center, Harvard Medical School, November 2003.

4. R. H. Hamilton, A. Pascual-Leone, and G. Schlaug, "Absolute Pitch in Blind Musicians," *Neuroreport*, 9 April 2004.

5. T. Kauffman, H. Theoret, and A. Pascual-Leone, "Braille Character Discrimination in Blindfolded Human Subjects," *Neuroreport*, 16 April 2002.

6. N. Sadato, A. Pascual-Leone, J. Grafman, M. P. Deiber, V. Ibanez, and M. Hallett, "Neural Networks for Braille Reading by the Blind," *Brain* (July 1998).

7. N. Sadato, A. Pascual-Leone, J. Grafman, M. P. Deiber, G. Dold, and M. Hallett, "Activation of the Primary Visual Cortex by Braille Reading in Blind Subjects," *Nature*, 11 April 1996.

8. Sam Keen, *Fire in the Belly: On Being a Man* (London: Piatkus, 1992).

CHAPTER 7

1. Diane K. Osborn, ed. *Reflections on the Art of Living: A Joseph Campbell Companion.*

2. Ibid.

3. Carl G. Jung, *Memories, Dreams, Reflections* (New York: Vintage, 1989).

4. George Bernard Shaw, recalled on his death, November 2, 1950.

5. Simon Buxton, *The Shamanic Way of the Bee* (Rochester, Vt.: 2004), 118.

6. Masaru Emoto, *The Hidden Messages in Water* (Hillsboro, Oreg.: Beyond Words Publishing, 2004).

7. Steve J. Ayan, "Right Brain May Be Wrong."

8. Ulrich Kraft, "Unleashing Creativity," *Scientific American Mind* 16, no. 1 (2005).

9. Alexander Carmichael, compiler, *Carmina Gadelica: Hymns and Incantations* (Edinburgh, Scotland: Floris Books, 1997).

CHAPTER 8

1. Viktor E. Frankl, *Man's Search for Meaning* (New York: Pocket Books, 1997).

2. Ibid.

3. Ibid.

4. Ibid.

5. Richard Gregory and Jean Wallace, "Recovery from Early Blindness: A Case Study," at www.richardgregory.org/papers/recovery_blind/contents.htm, reproduced from *Experimental Psychology Society Monograph* no. 2 (1963).

6. Ibid.

7. Ibid.

8. Ibid.

CHAPTER 9

1. Brian Keenan, *An Evil Cradling*.

Bibliography

Altman, I. and W. W. Haythorn. "The Ecology of Isolated Groups." *Behavioral Science* 12 (1967): 169–82, and I. Altman and W. W. Haythorn. "The Effects of Social Isolation and Group Composition on Performance." *Human Relations* 20 (1967): 313–39.

Angels in the Mirror: Vodou Music of Haiti. Roslyn, N.Y.: Ellipsis Arts, 1997.

Apuleius. *The Golden Ass.* Trans. E. J. Kenny. New York: Penguin Books, Penguin Classics new ed., 1999.

Ayan, Steve J. "Right Brain May Be Wrong." *Scientific American Mind* 16, no. 1 (2005).

Belli, Gioconda. *From Eve's Rib.* Trans. Steven F. White. Willimantic, Conn.: Curbstone Press, 1989.

Blacker, Carmen. *The Catalpa Bow.* London: George Allen and Unwin, 1975.

Blakeslee, Sandra. "Complex and Hidden Brain in the Gut Makes Cramps, Butterflies, and Valium." *New York Times,* 23 January 1996.

Buxton, Simon. *The Shamanic Way of the Bee: Ancient Wisdom and Healing Practices of the Bee Masters.* Rochester, Vt.: Destiny Books, 2004.

Carmichael, Alexander, compiler. *Carmina Gadelica: Hymns and Incantations.* Edinburgh, Scotland: Floris Books, 1997.

Davis, Wade. *One River.* New York: Simon and Schuster, 1997.

DelMonte, M. "Constructivist View of Meditation." *American Journal of Psychotherapy* 41, no. 2 (1987): 286–98.

Emoto, Masaru. *The Hidden Messages in Water.* Hillsboro, Oreg.: Beyond Words Publishing, 2004.

Frankl, Viktor E. *Man's Search for Meaning.* New York: Pocket Books, 1997.

Glouberman, Dina. *The Joy of Burnout: How the End of the World Can Be a New Beginning.* Makawao, Maui, Hawaii: Inner Ocean Publishing, 2003.

Gregg, Linda. *Too Bright to See & Alma.* Saint Paul, Minn.: Graywolf Press, 2002.

Gregory, Richard, and Jean Wallace. "Recovery from Early Blindness: A Case Study." At www.richardgregory.org/papers/recovery_blind/contents.htm, reproduced from *Experimental Psychology Society Monograph* no. 2 (1963).

Hamilton, R. H., A. Pascual-Leone, and G. Schlaug. "Absolute Pitch in Blind Musicians." *Neuroreport,* 9 April 2004.

Heaven, Ross. *The Journey to You: A Shaman's Path to Empowerment.* New York: Bantam, 2001.

———. *The Spiritual Practices of the Ninja: Mastering the Four Gates to Freedom.* Rochester, Vt.: Destiny Books, 2006.

———. *Vodou Shaman: The Haitian Way of Healing and Power.* Rochester, Vt.: Destiny Books, 2003.

Hebb, Donald O. *The Organization of Behavior.* Hoboken, N.J.: John Wiley and Sons, 1949.

Hutchinson, Michael. *The Book of Floating: Exploring the Private Sea.* Nevada City, Calif.: Gateways Books and Tapes, 2003.

Jung, Carl G. *Memories, Dreams, Reflections.* New York: Vintage, 1989.

Kauffman, T., H. Theoret, and A. Pascual-Leone. "Braille Character Discrimination in Blindfolded Human Subjects." *Neuroreport,* 16 April 2002.

Keen, Sam. *Fire in the Belly: On Being a Man.* London: Piatkus, 1992.

Keenan, Brian. *An Evil Cradling: The Five-Year Ordeal of a Hostage.* London: Random House, 1992.

Kraft, Ulrich. "Unleashing Creativity," *Scientific American Mind* 16, no. 1 (2005).

Lilly, John. *The Centre of the Cyclone.* London: Marion Boyars, 2001.

Male, Emile, and Dora Nussey. *The Gothic Image: Religious Art in France of the Thirteenth Century.* New York: HarperCollins, 1973.

Moore, Robert, and Douglas Gillette. *King, Warrior, Magician, Lover: Rediscovering the Archetypes of the Mature Masculine.* San Francisco: HarperSanFrancisco, 1999.

Moritsugu, Ken, Knight Ridder. "All Members of Primitive Tribe Survived Tsunami." *Yahoo! News,* 3 March 2005.

Morton Nance, R. *Gerlyver Noweth Kernewek.* Redruth, Cornwall, U.K.: Dyllansow Truran, 1990.

Osborn, Diane K., ed., *Reflections on the Art of Living: A Joseph Campbell Companion* (New York: HarperPerennial, 1991).

Pascual-Leone, A., and F. Torres. "Plasticity of the Sensorimotor Cortex Representation of the Reading Finger in Braille Readers." Bethesda, Md.: Human Cortical Physiology Unit, National Institute of Neurological Disorders and Stroke, National Institutes of Health.

Sadato, N., A. Pascual-Leone, J. Grafman, M. P. Deiber, G. Dold, and M. Hallett. "Activation of the Primary Visual Cortex by Braille Reading in Blind Subjects." *Nature,* 11 April 1996.

Sadato, N., A. Pascual-Leone, J. Grafman, M. P. Deiber, V. Ibanez, and M. Hallett. "Neural Networks for Braille Reading by the Blind." *Brain* (July 1998).

Snyder, Don J. *Of Time and Memory: My Parents' Love Story.* New York: Ballantine, 2001.

Somé, Malidoma Patrice. *Of Water and the Spirit: Ritual, Magic, and Initiation in the Life of an Afrrican Shaman.* New York: Penguin, 1995.

Sonnenmoser, Marion. "Friend or Foe?" *Scientific American Mind* 16, no. 1 (2005).

Sturgeon, John. *The Psychology of Isolation.* www.space.edu/LibraryResearch/undgrant.html.

Szegedy-Maszak, Marianne. "Your Unconscious Makes 95% of Your Decisions." *US News*.com, reprinted at www.mindpowernews.com/Unconscious.htm.

Theoret, H., L. Merabet, and A. Pascual-Leone. "Behavioral and Neuroplastic Changes in the Blind: Evidence for Functionally Relevant Cross-Modal Interactions." Laboratory for Magnetic Brain Stimulation, Department of Neurology, Beth Israel Deaconess Medical Center, Harvard Medical School, November 2003.

Wangyal, Tenzin, Rinpoche. *Wonders of the Natural Mind.* Ithaca, N.Y.: Snow Lion Publications, 2000.

Winkelman, Michael. *Shamanism: The Neural Ecology of Consciousness and Healing.* Westport, Conn.: Bergin & Garvey, 2000.

Darkness Visible and Other Workshops

Ross Heaven is a psychologist, therapist, and healer. He runs experiential and initiatory workshops in darkness: Darkness Visible and The Heart of Darkness, the latter a more advanced course for people who have already experienced darkness work. He is the author of *The Journey to You, Spirit in The City, Vodou Shaman,* and *The Spiritual Practices of the Ninja.* For details on these courses and other workshops led by Ross Heaven, visit: www.VodouShaman.com.

Simon Buxton is a shamanic teacher and practitioner and the author of *The Shamanic Way of the Bee.* He teaches Darkness Visible workshops, including The Heart of Darkness, as well as extended personal darkness retreats for individuals. Simon is the British faculty for Dr. Michael Harner's Foundation for Shamanic Studies and founder and director of The Sacred Trust, a UK-based educational organization dedicated to the teaching of practical shamanism for the modern world. He lives in England and teaches internationally. For details on Darkness Visible workshops and retreats and other teaching events with Simon Buxton, visit www.sacredtrust.org.

Both authors may be contacted in writing via the publisher. Send letters to the address on the copyright page of this book.